Railway Voices
'Inside'
Swindon Works

FIREWOOD CHOPPING MACHINE. OLD SAW MILL SWINDON   NEG M762 16
PHOTO'D 13. Nov. 1934

One of the benefits that came from working 'Inside' was the access to the 'perks' that came with it, 'perks' such as an allocation of coal, subsidised firewood (seen here being chopped from reclaimed timber and prepared in bundles by a young lad) as well as paint for the Company's 'ouses' (in the Company's colours, of course). Even better were the number of free 'passes' and subsidised 'privilege' tickets for train travel, initially over the GWR's own system but later over the other systems too. All this helped to establish the GWR's reputation of a 'grand paternalistic employer', however, as Professor Jack Simmons remarked: 'There was prudence in this as well as philanthropy. Good facilities were part of a policy to secure good service'. (Paul Williams' Hooper Collection).

Railway Voices 'Inside' Swindon Works

ROSA MATHESON

The
History
Press

'A better bunch of blokes you couldn't ever wish to work with.'

– Peter Reed

Front Cover Top:
'Works' Mad Rush' in Rodbourne Road – locals knew to stay
out of the way when the men were on their way home. (Paul
Williams' Hooper Collection)

Front Cover Bottom:
Outside the famous Works' main entrance in London Street
looking down Bristol Street towards St Mark's Church and the
Water Tower. (Paul Williams' Hooper Collection)

First published 2008

The History Press Ltd
The Mill, Brimscombe Port
Stroud, Gloucestershire, GL5 2QG
www.thehistorypress.co.uk

© Rosa Matheson, 2008

The right of Rosa Matheson to be identified as the Author
of this work has been asserted in accordance with the
Copyrights, Designs and Patents Act 1988.

ISBN 978 0 7524 4526 7

Typesetting and origination by The History Press Ltd.
Printed in Great Britain

Contents

Acknowledgements

Each time I start to write 'acknowledgements' I am increasingly aware of my good fortune in having so many kindly people who offer their expertise and enthusiastic support. Undoubtedly without their input my railway books could not have been as thoroughly and extensively investigated and brought to life as they have. If I cited everyone by name I would have to write another chapter but some groups and individuals need special mention.

Firstly thanks to all who dug deep into memories and shared their stories with me and those who went into attics and sheds to find forgotten photos and documents, especially all those of the Thursday Morning Club at the Community Centre and the two stalwarts there who organised my comings and goings, namely Ken Tanner and Dave Ellis. Thanks to all the volunteers in STEAM Museum of the GWR library who lent an ear and gave advice, to Elaine Arthurs, Archivist of STEAM, Roger Trayhurn and the staff at Swindon Reference Library. Individuals deserving of special mention are Ken Gibbs for opportunities for discussion and reading of work, Alan Philpott for guiding me to useful contacts and materials, John Plaister for his knowledge on clocks, Bob Townsend for legendary efforts on many aspects, John Walter for materials and offering advice along the way. A particular thanks to Paul Williams for use of his wonderful Hooper photographs, to David Hyde for photographs and guidance, to Graham Young for editorial assistance, and to all others who loaned precious personal photographs and mementoes. Special thanks to Lorna Dawes for all her kindness and help.

To anyone who should be thanked but has not been traceable, please accept my good intentions. To those who haven't made it into this book – there are more books coming.

An extra special thanks to my good friend Jack Hayward for his never-ending support and patience; for all the leg-work, research and data and photograph organisation and for finding me the most incredibly exciting stuff. I simply could not have managed without him.

A vote of thanks to my commissioning editor Amy Rigg for her kindly patience and professional management during the publication of this (and the previous two books), which has been beset by difficulties. As always, my last thanks to my family James, Hanna-Gael, Iainthe and Oona, and dear husband Ian, whose patience, encouragement and support kept me going through this surprisingly challenging enterprise.

Introduction

Isambard Kingdom Brunel is best remembered as the renowned engineer who built the Great Western Railway, but without any doubt his most important decision in respect to modern-day Swindon was to recommend the building of its world-acclaimed railway works on a then 'greenfield site'. Without that and its subsequent development it is doubtful whether the historic facts related in this book could ever have taken place. It has been said that if Paddington was the brain of the GWR, then Swindon Works was its beating heart. Sadly, it was not so in the era of British Rail.

'New Swindon' was born a railway town and its people were railway people – Great Western Railway people – even in the age of British Rail. In the beginning 'New Swindon' was the Works, the Company 'ouses and the nearby Swindon Junction Station with its inn, 'the Queen's Tap'; there was nothing else. Over the decades this frontier settlement grew into a town that became known worldwide because of its famous 'Works', its wonderful engines and carriages, its outstanding Superintendents and Chief Mechanical and Electrical Engineers, and the calibre of its craftsmen. The boast was 'if you had worked in Swindon Works you could get a job anywhere!' and that didn't just mean Britain, but anywhere in the world.

'The Works' was made up of many parts. Initially just a 'stabling and repair facility' for GWR's engines, it grew in activity and size until in 1878 Astills' *Swindon Local Guide* informed: 'There are three principal Departments in the Works, viz 1) The Locomotive Factories; 2) The Carriage and Wagon Works; 3) The Rolling Mills, occupying about 90 acres.' At its largest capacity, in the 1930s, it covered some 326 acres including the main lines running through them and the GWR boasted: 'Swindon Works comprise one of the largest railway establishments for the construction and repair of locomotives, carriages and wagons, in the world.' By the time of its closure in 1986, however, much had been knocked down, razed or sold off until only a few acres remained.

The story of 'the Works' or 'Inside' as it was known and called by Swindonians, is an industrial epic that stands on a par with any of the struggles and achievements of ancient or modern railway times as, from its very beginnings and through the whole of its life, it had to fight tooth and nail or 'steam and diesel' for its survival. Its story reflects the 'boom and bust' of railway fortunes both as a private company and as a nationalised enterprise. For 143 years the Works, through its people, heroically fought from one critical time to the next until the forces against

The Works was a place of many parts. It had many traditions and sayings. There was one particular saying in the Carriage Works, as the men would boast: 'It came in one end as a tree and went out the other as a carriage' The GWR would buy 'ship loads' of wood which would go through the various sawmills in the Works. It then had to be carefully stored to be 'seasoned' – nothing was 'kiln dried' then, before being put into use. During the Second World War, the GWR used their store of mahogany to build 'the Chariot', a two-man submarine. (Paul Williams' Hooper Collection)

it were too strong and it could no longer resist. On that sad historic day, 26 March 1986, when its hooter sounded at 4.30 p.m. for the last time, the part of Swindon which had been its *raison d'être* was no longer and was then consigned to history.

Whilst many books have been written about the Works, few, if any, have given a chance to those who worked in its railway workshops to have their voices heard in the telling of that story. This book uses their words and experiences to tell the good, the bad and the ugly of working 'Inside' from its beginning to its end.

Abbreviations

CM&EE – Chief Mechanical & Electrical Engineer
C&W – Carriage and Wagon
DMUs – Diesel Multiple Units
FTE – Fitter, Tuner, Erector
GWR – Great Western Railway
HG – Home Guard
WTS – Works' Training School

CHAPTER 1

Insiders

Swindon Works and New Swindon

The beginning of 'the Works' has entered into the mythology that is now part and parcel of the history of Swindon and its famous parent – the Great Western Railway. The starting point was the fact that the GWR needed a 'principal engine establishment' to stable and change-over their locomotives at a convenient point between Bristol and London. Isambard Kingdom Brunel, their young (just twenty-seven when appointed), flamboyant Engineer, and the even younger Daniel Gooch (just twenty-one), the first Locomotive Superintendent at Swindon Works, were given the task of finding a situation for such an establishment. Gooch records in his diary: 'Mr Brunel and I went to look at the ground, then only green fields, and he agreed with me as to its being the best place.' The 'romantic' story suggests that the site of the Works was decided 'on the toss of a sandwich' which was purportedly part of their picnic lunch. It tells that where the sandwich fell determined where the new enterprise would rise. It is fact and not fiction, however, that Gooch wrote to Brunel in September 1840 suggesting that, having put his mind to the task of the best site and having 'studied the convenience of the Great Western only' (i.e. not considering the convenience of the workers and families who would have to live there) the best point lay at Swindon at the junction of the Cheltenham and Great Western Union Railway and the nearby Wilts & Gloucester Canal. The Company agreed and gave its decision:

> To provide an Engine establishment at Swindon, commensurate with the wants of the Company, where a change of engines may be advantageously made, and the trains stopped for the purposes of the passengers taking refreshments … The Establishment there would also comprehend the large repairing shops for the Locomotive Department.

So it was that New Swindon came to be built on what was, in modern terminology, a greenfield site. Old Swindon, the seat of the Goddard family, lay a good trudge across fields and up the steep hill to the south. The distance between Old and New Swindon existed not just in physical geography, but also on a social, cultural, and even intellectual level. Tradition versus modernity.

Old Swindon was 'old country', its people, thinking and economies based in agricultural habits and customs. New Swindon was the new industrial age, new libertine thinking, new species of workers. In epic terms it was Old World versus New. World commenced on building the new factory in 1841. Gooch's diary tells us that machinery at the Works was 'started up' on 28 November 1842 and that the factory began full work on 2 January 1843. By 1843 the Works employed 423 men, of which seventy-two were 'highly skilled engineers'.

Hand-in-hand with the story of the Works goes the story of 'New Swindon', as, obviously, there was little point in having a wonderful factory, if one didn't have the people to work in it. Unfortunately, the GWR decided to build the Works in the middle of nowhere, and therefore:

> the circumstances rendered it necessary to arrange for the building of cottages etc., for the residence of the many persons employed in the service of the Company … The Company are to provide land for the cottages, and to secure to Builders a fixed rent upon lease, which rent will of course be reimbursed by the tenants of the cottages.[1]

The village was started in 1842 and extended in fits and starts over the next five years. Richard Jefferies describes it in his *History of Swindon* (1896) as 'flat and damp in situation'. The first terraces of cottages built of local stone formed a symmetrical pattern around a central square and were more pleasing to the eye than to inhabit. The fronts, with small gardens facing on to the railway line, were more elegant and attractive than the functional backs where the small backyard contained a dusthole and a privy with access in the wall for removing 'night-soil'. Edward Snell, who came to New Swindon to seek his fortune in the railway world of opportunity, wrote of the village in March 1843 in his now famous diary:

> A precious place it is at present, not a knocker or scraper in the whole place! [This was an essential requirement and usually provided in those times of mud roads and footpaths]. Most of the houses very damp and containing only two rooms, not a cupboard or a shelf … and the unfortunate inhabitants obliged to keep the grub in the bedrooms.[2]

From its beginning there was serious overcrowding in the village as house building, despite Jefferies' comment that 'houses were built at a rate that astonished the country', could not keep up with demand. As early as 1845 Daniel Gooch wrote to J. Hammond, Brunel's assistant, urging a speedy completion of new cottages as those available were now housing anything from ten to twenty people in the two rooms and when the day shift emptied their beds the night shift took up occupation.[3]

At its beginnings New Swindon was very much a 'frontier town'. The nearest shops were across the canal, a trudge through fields, across stiles and up a long steep hill to Old Town. There was no school, no church, no place for recreation. When Daniel Gooch was considering the requirements of this site the only drawback he noted was, as he wrote in a letter to Brunel on 13 September 1840, 'the bad supply of water', which he believed was of no real consequence as 'we have the canal'. On commencement of the building of the Works and village, provision for clean water was made only for the Works not the village; provision for the houses came via the canal, the same canal into which the privies from the cottages and other effluent would be emptied. Snell wrote: 'Not a drop of water to be had but what comes from the tenders or out of

View of New Swindon, *c.*1876. From left to right: St Mark's Church (consecrated 1845) with Park House in front (1876); railway village Bristol Street Water Tower (1871); Mechanics' Institute (1855), with the GWR hospital in front (1871). Centre ground: the Wilts & Berks Canal with boat; fields in foreground now the town shopping centre (as identified by Jack Hayward).

the ditches and what little we do get is a thick as mud … not fit for a jackass to drink.'[4] Supply of the water was strictly controlled. On 27 November 1856, John Fraser, assistant manager, informed the villagers:

> It having been reported to Mr [W.] Gooch that there had been great waste of water in the village from various causes but especially from the Taps being left open, Notice is hereby given that if this be continued then the water will be only turned on for one hour each day.

For over twenty years proper clean drinking water had to be purchased from water carriers who brought in supplies from the Wroughton Road spring near Old Town. A letter in the *Swindon Advertiser* in 1867 signed 'Yours respectively, A Mechanic', thanks the Local Board for voting £27 towards 'securing a poor fellow on this side of the canal a supply of wholesome water instead of that impure and unwholesome liquid … which was derived from the canal.' The lack of a proper clean water supply, the multiple 'shared' accommodation, the keeping of 'fowls, ducks, rabbits or any other nuisances' (as stated in Medical Fund Minutes of September

1853) in the backyards to supplement food supplies, the churned-up muddy footpaths and roadways, all gave the feeling of a 'frontier camp' for a number of years, albeit an architecturally well designed and laid out 'camp'! It was all to have sad and dire consequences for the village inhabitants as illnesses such a tuberculosis (known as consumption as it 'consumed the lungs') and outbreaks of cholera and typhus were not uncommon and the high mortality rate struck at all ranks, especially amongst old and young; even as late as 1880 when, in November, there were fifteen funerals, ten of which were children.[5] Such conditions affected and moulded the character of the village inhabitants, bringing to them a toughness and resilience.

The everyday comfort and quality of life for the village inhabitants improved slowly over many years due mainly to the energies of the workers themselves but with the co-operation and support of the local officers of the company assisting and mediating on their behalves. On such a basis came the Mechanics' Institute, the fee-paying school and the church, all establishing the GWR's reputation as a 'paternalistic' employer on a grand scale. Trevor Cockbill, a local socialist historian, and Jackie Pierce, in her BA thesis, claim that the real credit for 'paternalistic activity' actually lies with the early residents of New Swindon themselves. A good example of this is in the setting up of Swindon's Mechanics' Institution. PRO archive records show how the GWR recorded in 1843 'a subscription of £30, to be laid down in books for the use of the New Swindon Mechanics' Institution Library.' 'The Institute', as it was fondly called by the locals, gives in its first Annual Report of January 1845 a 'short account of its formation and rise to the present period' and records: 'as along ago as September 1843 a few members opened a library, with a small number of books a few kind friends gave them, and [here is GWR's input] others that were purchased with a small sum of money that had accumulated from fines in the hands of the Company,' i.e. the Company gave the men not GWR money, but monies that it had already taken from them in punitive fines. In fact, from its beginnings the GWR, always aware that it was 'holding the purse on behalf of shareholders', practised an economic-centred style of paternalism that showed a stern, sometimes even puritanical, face demanding a good return for any investment or outlay. For the GWR it was never a simple matter of benevolence, more a mutually beneficial partnership of undertaking.

By 1847 rapid expansion, albeit with one or two hiccups on the way, had increased the number of workmen to 1,800,[6] but these were difficult times on the railways, Railway Mania was running out of steam, and this was another crucially critical time for the Works and its workmen. The directors ordered strict economic measures resorting to day-rates rather than piece-rates and drastically reduced the scale of operations and men. Edward Snell confessed in his diary, 'when I was twenty-one I calculated on making a fortune by the time I was thirty, but have made little headway.' He had made steady progress to become head draughtsman and then on to Assistant Works Manager under Archibald Sturrock, but in 1848 his progress was halted. He recorded: 'work getting slacker and slacker … the men making only four and a half days a week and a great number of them sacked.'[7] Gooch argued strongly against such drastic action stating:

Swindon has been designed and built to employ 1,800-2,000 men, and all the arrangements of tools and shops have been made to employ that number of men to the best advantage, and are, therefore, not so well adapted for our present diminished numbers, the fixed charges or shop expenses are in consequence heavier than they would be in a plan better proportioned to the work to be done. Any work that can be obtained will, therefore, assist to reduce

Because of the lack of accommodation in New Swindon the GWR introduced 'Special Trains, Morning and Evening' as early as July 1853 for those workmen who resided at Steventon and later in August that year for those in Wootton Bassett too. Over 100 years later John Charlesworth's Free Pass enabled him to ride on the Workman's Train from Purton.

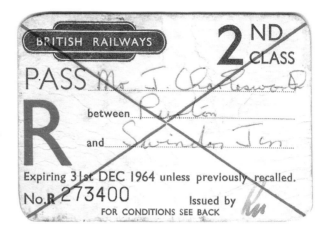

these expenses; in fact we have the means at Swindon if we have the work of earning a manufacturers' prices at least £20,000 p.a.

It was to no avail. Almost half the workforce was dismissed and only one hundred were retained for work on new engines.[8] Many of those discharged left the area. Snell decided to seek his fortune in Australia. There was great difficulty and distress in the railway village. Touched by the plight of men who were laid off and by the valiant efforts of those who were still in work to support those discharged, particularly in their medical costs, Daniel Gooch wrote a letter of supplication to the Secretary of the Company movingly requesting permission to provide some medical assistance to the men in these most difficult times. It was to have significant and far-reaching outcomes. The GWR, recognising the benefits to the Company in this, agreed that Dr S. Rea (brother of Minard Rea, Works Manager), the attending Surgeon, be allowed his Company house rent free 'in consideration of his professionally attending all those to whom accidents may occur in the Works or on the company's premises,'[9] and so in 1847 the now famous GWR Medical Fund Society came into being 'to provide medicine and attendance to those employed by the GWR Company at Swindon'.

It was also laid down that every employee must 'subscribe a rateable portion of their wages' to the Medical Fund and join the Sick Fund Society as a condition of employment, becoming the first company in the country to do so and, at Minard Rea's suggestion, the GWR agreed that the contributions would be deducted from wages. From this humble beginning the Medical Fund went on to provide for every medical need – doctor, dentist, optician, pharmacist, accident hospital, subscriptions to three other main hospitals and convalescent homes – and a good deal more: washing baths, Turkish baths, and swimming baths were all provided by the Society, even a barber. Mrs Joyce Murgatroyd's uncle, Walter Bezer, worked as such. 'He used to shave the men in the hospital, or cut their hair. Sometimes he had to go to their homes to do so.' So good was this extensive provision of services and care that it was the envy of all those who did not work for the GWR and it was one of the great perks that attracted people to work for and stay with the Company, even at times when, as Mrs Saunders[10] said, 'they could have got higher wages, i.e. money in their pockets, elsewhere.' It is claimed that the Medical

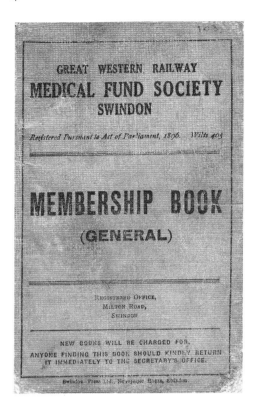

Left: The Mechanics' Institute Medical Fund Society provided doctors, opticians, dentists, dispensary, tickets of admission to specialist hospitals and convalescent homes, an emergency local hospital, baths, invalid chairs and a hearse (originally a horse-drawn shillibier but later a motor vehicle). 'Insiders' used to say they were 'looked after from the cradle to the grave'.

Below: Many shops had their own 'benefit' societies which would be run and administered by their own shop committee. Albert Edward George Dawes belonged to one in J Shop (Iron Foundry) which assisted members 'in ordinary sickness or sickness caused by accident'.

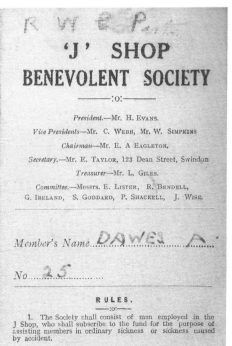

Fund Society provided Aneurin Bevan, Labour Minister of Health, with a working 'role model' for the National Health Service, the birth of which on 5 July 1948 saw the demise of the Fund. The Sick Fund and the Medical Fund were not the only funds that the men contributed to, there were several others, some limited to the different shops. Such funds carried on even when formal State assistance was instigated via the National Insurance Stamp contribution. Lorna Dawes still has her father's membership book to the 'J Shop (Iron Foundry) Benevolent Society' for 1942–1944 where membership was restricted to only those in J Shop.

The early railway workers and inhabitants of New Swindon were initially held to be of rowdy and unsound character. Surprising really when you look at the first skilled workers who came as settlers, but it has to be remembered that New Swindon was, initially, merely a collection of people from different parts of the country; the 1851 Census returns for Taunton Street alone identifies immigrants from Scotland, Cumberland, Durham, Northumberland and Smithfield, London.[11] Catell and Falkner identify twenty-two different birthplaces outside of Wiltshire plus a non-specific 'other' category. These people came with their own cultural identities, practices and habits, both good and bad, and made the best of a very difficult situation. Their first energies had to be directed into meeting day-to-day needs and so it took some time for a collective community identity and responsibility to emerge, which the church, through its pastoral role, and the new school then helped develop. Another factor to remember is the young age of most of the men and their families, even 'the Management' – Gooch, Sturrock, Rea – were all rather young men. 'Railways' was a new industry and it attracted a new breed of men. Men willing to be bold and daring, willing to push boundaries, willing to upheave themselves and their families and take a chance! They were spirited men and women; people with 'something about them' (a phrase that is constantly used by those speaking about people in the Works). One of the first immigrant families to arrive in 1842 was that of Henry Appleby, who became Superintendent of the Locomotive Dept. Being such an important man, Henry would have had priority for any newly built accommodation. The Appleby family is believed to have lived at 1 Bristol Street, the first of the cottages built, but by 1865 is recorded as living at 13 Oxford Street. The first wedding recorded for New Swindon is that of Miss Ann Pavey of Wroughton who married Dr Stuart Keith Rea, the first surgeon appointed to the Railway Works. Their marriage took place at the new church of St Mark's on 21 February 1846.[12]

In the beginnings there was little or nothing in terms of entertainment or relaxation for the villagers, apart from the local taverns and the 'demon drink'. With accommodation full to bursting, it was probably easier to stop out and drink with one's mates. Business was also transacted in the ale houses, contractors taking their men there for the wages payout. Folklore has it that this was part of a wicked plan to get them drunk and then, whilst befuddled, pay them less generously than they should have been paid. It also has to be borne in mind that drinking water was an expensive commodity and not easy to come by, and beer was cheap. Cheap beer and cheap gin were not only 'mother's ruin' but the cause of many fracas and public nuisances in the 'new town' and, probably, accidents in the Works. Richard Jefferies wrote: 'the workmen at this factory enjoyed an unpleasant notoriety for mischief and drunkenness.' The local paper was often reporting on such incidents brought before the magistrates. Undoubtedly the railway villagers were a troublesome lot for the Company. On several occasions Works' Manager Minard Rea had to lay down the law to them:

Henry Appleby had come down from Newcastle in 1837 accompanying the engine *North Star*. He was one of the first workers to come to 'New Swindon'. His wife, Elizabeth, gave birth to a daughter, Ann, known to her family ever after as 'Annie Appleby, Queen of the Cottages' (details in letter to author from Mrs Ellen Newcombe whose grandfather, George Henry Wall, lived at 4 Bristol Street and worked in the Works in the 1860s). The address given on the birth certificate dated 23 October 1842 was 'The Station, Swindon'. Henry, despite being only able to put his 'mark' on his daughter's certificate, rose to be 'Superintendent of the Locomotive Department' (as identified on his daughter's birth certificate), specifically the Running Shed.

May 1853 – The following Cottage Chimneys were on fire on the following dates & attention is called to a change in the agreement signed by the tenant of the Company –
'And if I wilfully or by any negligence set fire to my Chimney, I will pay the Company the sum of 5/- for every such offence.' In future this policy will be carried strictly into operation. Cottage Chimneys on fire.
May 7th 1853 – 47 Exeter Street
May 9th 1853 – 14 Taunton St.
May 9th 1853 – 32 Bath St.
Signed M Rea.

The 'village' took a long time to settle and in 1855 there were still those who were causing great annoyance. This time it is William Gooch (Daniel Gooch's brother), now Works Manager, who writes:

In calling the attention of the workmen to yesterday's disgraceful and riotous proceedings in the Works and the Village, leading in one case to the destruction of property, I have to request that all men who value the peace, good order and respectability of the village will use every endeavour to preserve the same.

He goes on to urge the residents to report 'the leaders' to him. Four years later, in January 1859, 'mischief' was still a problem, this time inside the Works. Mr Gooch is driven to post an uncommonly high reward in respect of 'sabotage':

£2 REWARD

Whereas some evil disposed person or persons put a piece of
gas pipe into the Exhaust part of the Prometheus Engine between
Thursday and Saturday the 20th and 22nd inst., the above regard
will be given to any person who will give such information as will
lead to any conviction of the offender or offenders.

Whether this was an accident or deliberate malicious action, an unrestrained young boy's vandalism or an apprentice's prank is, of course, not known, but it exemplifies the nature of the unruliness that prevailed at these times. As late as 1865 those now called 'the Rough Band' were still causing annoyance, if not to the villagers, decidedly to the Management!

F.G. Richens describes the activities of the 'rough bands' in the *Great Western Railway Magazine* (1934) as a version of an old Wiltshire tradition called 'wosset hunting'. In a small village knowing everybody's business came as a matter of course, so that: 'news of any domestic troubles or discreditable incidents came quickly to the ears of the rough band leaders … who regarded themselves as the defenders of the public good name.' They would arm themselves with anything that could be made to make a loud noise – frying pans, kettles, musical instruments – and play marching through the village with as many as 'two hundred persons taking part'. Halting outside the offending abode, they would 'serenade the victims for the rest of the evening,' returning evening after evening until 'something else distracted the attention of the ringleaders'. Now it is Mr Samuel Carlton, who writes and informs villagers that: 'persons will be set to watch' so that if anyone employed at the Works is seen 'aiding and abetting … such disgraceful proceedings … they will be discharged.' Yet whilst all this mayhem was going on, there were some villagers who did their best to civilise their 'camp'. Trevor Cockbill writes of the Institute's 'New Swindon Horticultural and Flower Exhibition' that took place in 1854 and of the winners of the 'best kept front gardens' and of the 'cleanest back premises' entries as well as those in the 'produce' classes, with Works' Manager and fellow tenant Minard Rea almost sweeping the board with first prize in the 'best dish of peas, the best white cabbage, the best six sticks of celery, and the best six carrots,' but only second prize for his parsnips![13]

The numbers in the Works and in New Swindon continued to grow until in 1861 Old Swindon was finally outstripped by its thrusting younger neighbour, managing only 2,089 to New Swindon's staggering 4,167.[14] The contractor, Mr Thomas Ellis, believed to have designed, constructed and then managed the Rail Mills from 1861–1866, had brought with him from Wales new people with new skills and a new language, adding another ingredient into the rich community mix. These Welsh incomers were invited to set up home in Brunel's 'model lodging house' on Faringdon Road, started in 1849 but not finished until 1855. 'The Barracks' as it became known, was originally built as accommodation for single men and its small separate bedrooms were quickly converted into units, but still with shared communal spaces, for the new Welsh families. Inspector Henry Haynes of the Swindon Local Board of Health was not impressed, for, like the village houses, whilst striking outside, the inside left a great deal to be desired. He wrote to the Board in August 1866: 'I consider this building in its present state quite unfit for human habitation and dangerous to the health of the district … The building is in a dirty, filthy state all over and in a very bad state of repair.'[15] One wonders how much the Board squirmed, the principals amongst them all being GWR officials, the others local companies, many of whom were dependent upon the goodwill of the GWR. On this occasion they did their duty and initiated legal proceedings against the GWR in order to force it to carry out improvements. It was obviously not a situation that its new tenants could endure for long or in harmonious accord and soon the incomers were seeking to put down more comfortable and permanent roots. Ellis had formed a building company amongst his men and from 1864 erected a small 'settlement' of cottages nearby called Cambrai Place, and Baptist Chapel in 1866, which became a 'little Wales' in Swindon.

After their shaky and somewhat volatile beginnings the workmen slowly developed a solid reputation based on self-improvement, self-help, and work of the highest standards. Writing in 1875 Jefferies noted the 'strong *esprit de corps*' and superior intelligence of this 'small nation of workers, this army of the hammer, lathe and drill,' remarking: 'where one book is read in agricultural districts, fifty are read in the vicinity of the factory' and judged that: 'they are probably higher in their intellectual life than a large proportion of the so-called middle classes.' The books these mechanics read so avidly were available through the Institute's library which had been started up 'in a large room in the Works' in September 1843 with just a handful of members to give the workmen some distraction, other than the frequenting of local pubs, as well as some recreation and improvement through knowledge. One of its earliest activities apart from the sharing of books was the provision of newspapers and journals, the extent and range of which was staggering. An article in the *Swindon Advertiser* in 1855 lists almost forty ranging from *The Times, Edinburgh News, Wiltshire Independent, Punch, Journal of the Society of Arts, Family Friend, Eliza Cook's Journal, Temperance Herald* and *Bradshaw's Railway Guide*, fulfilling 'the Institute's' aim of 'disseminating useful knowledge and encouraging rational amusement amongst all classes of people employed by the Great Western Railway [for] the benefits to married men and their families from the perusal of the books.' From these small beginnings it quickly flourished. The Institute's own building, the physical focal point of New Swindon, was formally opened in May 1855 and modified and enlarged in 1892 and 1930. It was to become the heart of all social and cultural activity for the Works' men and their families. Reading and recreation, concerts and lectures, music making and dramatic productions, self-improvement and instruction, annual dinners and teas, fêtes and excursions – 'the Institute' was where it all happened. Educational courses for men, boys and young women were laid on and well attended. A variety of subjects for study was available under its umbrella. By the early 1890s the Institute had a membership of upwards of 6,000 members and a library of 1,700 volumes, which increased to over 50,000 volumes by 1932.

By this time the reputation of New Swindon had completely turned around and this essentially working-class town was then always to maintain a solidly 'middle-class' attitude in terms of 'respectability'. Writing of the 1930s and '40s, Trevor Cockbill remarks: 'Such "respectability" was not held to be achieved by ostentatious behaviour or flamboyant acquisition, but by subdued modesty [and] almost all the people seemed prepared to sacrifice virtually everything they possessed in pursuit of "respectability".' A good example of such 'sacrifice' is the story of Mrs S, who, before she started work at the GWR in the 1940s, was employed as a machinist in Compton's clothing manufacturers. Her pay was low and her father's wages at the Works not really enough to keep the family adequately. 'It was a great struggle for my mother. My father would not allow her to work or to take in work.' In order to help ease the difficulties, Mrs S would stay behind for half an hour after her usual work-time and do the sweeping up for extra money. This casual arrangement worked very well until it came to the ears of her father via the 'community grapevine'. He was furious and forbade his daughter to carry on. 'He said it was not respectable and showed the family in a bad light.' Mrs S believed that she, her mother and the family paid a high price with their struggles to maintain her father's 'railway pride' and need for respectability that came as being part and parcel of the GWR, part and parcel of 'the Works' and part and parcel of being a 'railway family' which had to be maintained at all costs by those who worked 'Inside'.

Inside

'Inside' was the name given to Swindon Works by its workers and their families. The term was appropriate because the Works was virtually contained inside an embracing wall surround that had been built up over the decades. Entry to 'Inside' was via carefully guarded gates or tunnel entrances. On emerging from the famous tunnel off London Street, it was like emerging into another world which has been described by some who worked there as 'like a town inside a town … it had its own roads and big buildings … it was like a little town really.' 'Inside' was a place separate from the outside world, where, even in the 1970s, the impact had not diminished, and this feeling was just as intense for young apprentice Gordon Dickinson as he 'visited', anticipating his move from the Works Training School to 'Inside':

> Toward the end of the year it was announced that we would be going through the tunnel and emerge in the 'real world' (Inside) for a tour of what was to become our workplace for at least the next four years. This, for me, was probably the most exciting day of my whole apprenticeship … I was not disappointed … It was fantastic … The enormity of everything, the sounds, the smells, the machines, the buildings, but most of all the men. I think there were about 3,000 of them, every shape and size imaginable, all wearing blue or brown overalls, some were covered in oil and grease. They were welding, sparking, flashing, banging, hammering, screwing, shouting, laughing, smoking fags, drinking tea, reading *The Sun* (smart new paper at the time). We saw white hot molten metal being poured in the foundry by men drenched in sweat, with forearms that Hercules would have envied; we watched the enormous buffer springs being formed from red hot lengths of steel rod being fed into coiling machine and then dipped into oil which let out a wonderful bubbling hiss followed by a thick cloud of white steam that rose high into the vast open space above, spot-lit by shafts of light coming in through the tall windows, then explode silently and disappear into nothing as it hit the roof high above us. These springs would then be put into the spring tester, a solid gigantic hammer that would come crashing down to test the quality of true spring metal … As we watched I'm certain that we were all thinking the same thought … 'bugger getting my hand in the way of that thing!' We watched amazed as single men levered coaches, weighing tonnes [tons], almost effortlessly along the shiny tracks that lay in row after row, stretching from one end to the

other of these impressive old buildings. We stood in awe at their skill as they then put wooden radius-shaped wedges between the wheels and tracks to bring these gorgeous huge silent monsters to a smooth halt as they met buffer to buffer then sprang back slowly and came to a satisfying halt. It was a lot to take in.

We can see from Gordon's description that 'Inside' was a man's place; a place bulging with masculine values and masculinity; a place full of machismo and male pride. If young men found it overwhelming, imagine how much more so it would have been for young women, yet a small part of 'Inside' (admittedly on its outside edge in London Street) was, amazingly, women's domain. In the early 1870s the newly constructed Carriage Department was, according to its 'Superintendent' Mr J. Holden, struggling to recruit skilled workmen owing to the fact there were virtually no employment opportunities in Swindon for young women and girls. Such was the problem that Joseph Armstrong, the first Superintendent of the Locomotive and Carriage & Wagon Works, took the bold decision to provide a workshop fitted up for this purpose in the 'upholstery department of the Carriage Works' and in 1874 the first handful of girls was taken on.

Alphabetical Register of Workmen CARRIAGE DEP: Oct 1877–1907

Name	Entered	Left	Job
1874			
Mary Burge	15/8/74	13/11/80	Ling Wm [lining woman]
Cecilia Fullond	18/7/74	—	POL [polisher]
Mary Isles	15/8/74	13/11/80	POL
Jessie McGregor	15/8/74	24/12/78	POL
Martha Ribson	15/12/74	23/12/80	POL
1875			
Caroline Shaw	3/11/75	1/7/87	POL
Isabella Turnbull	23/6/75	—	POL
Sarah Jane Sanders	16/7/75	10/10/78	POL
Harriet Smith	16/7/75	5/4/78	POL
Rachel Smith	13/8/75	12/4//90	POL
Ellen Dempsey	2/11/75	—	POL

Surprisingly, rather than in a female 'sewing' capacity, most of the first girls were taken on to do polishing. Whilst polishing was a 'womanly' skill and occupation in the home, 'French polishing' was a skilled artisan's job, yet, despite the fact that this was seen as purely 'temporary' employment between leaving school and woman's rightful destiny – marriage – the girls were taught how to 'pickle' and strip, colour and tone and finally polish and 'finish' anything that was made of wood in the train: doors, panels, window frames, luggage-rack poles, wood partitions, even toilet seats. The girls were mostly aged between fifteen and twenty when joining, although one, Alice Holliday, is identified on the 'Register of *Men*' (my italics) as being born on 24 February 1880, and on entering the Works in November 1893 was aged just thirteen.

The 'handful' of women taken on in 1874 quickly grew in number and their range of work was extended so that a booklet entitled *The Great Western Railway, The Town and Works of Swindon* (1892) informs that: 'About 100 women in all are employed; some French Polishing; others working sewing-machines, making nets, trimming and various other descriptions of work in connection with the carriage trimming.'

Mindful of their 'moral responsibilities' and of the reputation of these young Victorian girls, the GWR 'carefully studied … the arrangement for the comfort of the women' so that they were 'provided with a separate entrance and left at somewhat different hours from the men'. Rather than 'annual dinners' as with other departments, the 'females' (which the Company's magazine constantly referred to them as) had 'annual teas' after which they provided their own entertainments in the form of singing, dancing and small dramatic 'playlets'. These female workers were also allowed membership of 'the Institute' as a small item in the AGM of 1895 highlights. A committee member, Mr Phillips, reports of:

the necessity of providing a female ward [in the Accident Hospital] as the females employed in the Works … paid their quota to the funds … but did not receive the same benefits as the male members. In the event of a female accident they had to be taken to the Victoria Hospital and this would be considered a disgrace to the Society.

These female workers established a tradition that lasted way beyond the demise of the GWR. They became part of the 'fabric' of the C & W even to becoming part of the 'initiation' of young boys, as Roy Blackford ruefully remembers:

If you ever went on George Drew's gang you'd get it. Just across the traversing yards was the lady polishers. Now, once they got a young lad who was a bit green, hadn't been on the job five minutes and didn't know any different, old George would give you some piecework order or something and say, 'Oh take this over to the lady polisher would you' and her bench would be right at the end of the shop, and you'd have to walk up all the way through. The ladies and the girls had their benches each side of the gangway, so you would walk up through and there'd be a few catcalls. You'd give the lady the paper and she would be smiling and say, 'yeah I've got nothing at the moment' so you'd go to go back, but when you turned round all these girls had closed into the gangway, hadn't they. The gangway was all filled up, they'd all be in there and you had to run-the-gauntlet. Well I say no more. You only got caught once. You didn't go again.

Whilst Armstrong had hoped for many shops for women's employment in the Works, it wasn't until the war years that women made further entry into other workshops. During the First World War their entry was resisted on the basis of there being no 'facilities' for them in the workshops, and in truth there were none, but also because of the intense antagonism of the railway companies, the unions and even the men towards women doing men's work, as it threatened men's jobs and men's pay. The heavy demands of the Second World War, however, meant that women had to be accommodated and the men had to adapt to these new 'Insiders'. Recruited and conscripted female war workers faced a mixed reception from the men on the shop floor, from open hostility to resigned acceptance, yet for most of the women the experience of working 'Inside', whilst being difficult and challenging in many ways, was also life-enriching and rewarding. They got to do things they would never have otherwise done, for which they were paid a 'man's rate', albeit the lowest rate, as well as playing a valued part in 'winning the war' whilst doing so. Mrs Vera Russell learned to drive a trailer tractor: 'This was good. I loved it. You had to load, couple up and deliver. I could eventually back three trailers altogether.' Vera remembers there were eight women with her all learning to drive different vehicles for use inside and outside the Works. 'In the beginning they [the men] didn't like us, but then, when they got to know us, it was like they protected us in a way, looked out for us.' Mrs Violet Holder worked on an overhead crane, No.1 crane in the Boiler Shop: 'The first time I went up I thought I'd never come down I was so scared, it seemed so high. The foreman came up with me and showed me the controls and George Miles was the man on the floor, who put on the chains and gave me the signals. Once I got used to it I really enjoyed it and the money seemed a lot compared to Wills.' Mike White remembers that his Aunty Mary, born 1923, went in the Blacksmiths Shop in 1939, aged just sixteen, where she stayed for the whole war period.

   Swindon Works was heavily involved in munitions production in both world wars. In the First World War it was the only type of other work the women war recruits did, but in the Second World War many started on munitions before being transferred over to 'railway work proper'. Mrs Ada Werrell started in 24 Shop (Carriage Builders) in 1941:

   I was on a lathe turning shells, munitions. There weren't many of us there, about twenty-four altogether, mostly women apart from the chargeman, Doug Mundan, our setter and the Foreman, Mr Ashley Walker. We weren't there for more than a year because they dismantled the lathes to be sent to America and then we were taken out and put into various shops.

Many of these female war recruits already had family connections 'Inside', fathers, brothers, uncles, husbands and boyfriends, which made it easier for them to fit in and be accepted, but for the women that came from further afield, the men found them to be something of a novelty, sometimes even a challenge. 'We had some girls from London, and they gave as good as they got', remembers Mr X. 'You didn't want to get on the wrong side of their tongue.' Mrs Werrell worked alongside some of these girls:

> Later I went to AM (Machine) Shop at Rodbourne Road. I was on railway work then. I was shifted over to a milling machine. Some of the girls who had been called up were from Devon, some girls had come up from Bristol as well. Ruby Godwin, in her early twenties, was on my gang. Phil (Fortune) Fry was in there. On the lathe next to me was the sisters Grace and Maud Jamieson from London. They'd been bombed out. We had a girl, real modern for those days, Blondie, she was a scream. The men used to wolf whistle. She was plump and proud of it. She married George. Hilda was on a small walking crane. She was getting on then. Ella, Win, Grace and Maud were in the Great Western until after the war finished and then they were took over to where they do the upholstery.

The end of the war spelled the end of women's accepted time in the workshops and most, although not all, like Mrs Violet Holder who stayed on till 1949, were quickly laid off in line with the Government's and Union's Pre-War Agreements. Whilst many women were only too pleased to be released from such arduous work in such atrocious conditions, others confessed that given the choice, they would loved to have stayed, citing it as 'the best time of my life'.

'The Laundry' was another area which became 'women's domain' within the Works. Ten women started in 1893 and the number grew to over fifty in the new purpose-built laundry of 1938. Clive Wilson's Aunty 'Al' (Alice Edmonds) worked in the old laundry. Clive, when a lad, used to go in to see her and remembers how dark and dingy it was in there, full of steam and the heavy smell of soap. He tells how firemen and engine drivers would drop off their filthy overalls to be de-greased, washed and ironed and 'pay' Aunty Alice with produce from their allotments.

Post-war and post-Nationalisation recruitment problems, however, meant that for a few short years, women were once again actually recruited into the workshops. Pam Pinnegar, who worked in F1 and F2 (Blacksmith) Shops from 1948 until the mid-1950s, was one of these. Pam's sister Peggy joined her and the other women there. Pam recalls that the women established their own routines within that of the shop, which were accepted by the men:

We spent a lot of time in the restroom when we weren't needed because there were times when there were heats or when they just worked on the anvils, when they made hand tools without using the hammers. We used to wash or perm our hair then and the smell was something terrible. It was in-between jobs we could do it. We did lots of things like that. We always walked up the town at lunch-time, do a bit of shopping or just to get out, even though it was still on rations. Then after a few years things got quiet. We had to go because there wasn't the work about. Some of the hammers were closed down then. [They later closed the F1 Shop] We got made redundant. We weren't give much notice. We knew it was coming. We were replaced by men then.

Peggy says:

I have lots of good memories of F Shop. I was very happy. Lots of friendship. If the blacksmith did something wrong like, all the others would cheer and shout. We'd all help each other. Pam and I walked across to the Carriage side to get the polish to polish the foreman's office. That took us all afternoon. I had worked in Wills factory before. It was very strict in there. Going 'Inside' it was a lot more easy. We were on a man's wage: £8.90. A flat rate. No bonus. I worked at the aircraft factory previous to that for £4.50 so that was the difference. A man's job for a man's wage and a Free Pass, of course. That was the incentive to go 'Inside'.

It is easy to see that for the workers and their families 'Inside' was more than just a physical place, it was an entity imbued with values and practices that impacted on every aspect of their lives. Every part of their life – work, social, cultural, political, even, it is true to say, their hopes, dreams and fears – all were affected by it. 'Inside' affected 'outside' and these railway people liked to live their whole lives within the railway community so, not unsurprisingly, around the Works there lived few who were not connected with it. Jack Harber, whose father was a GWR fitter and volunteer fireman in the Works, lived in the railway village in Exeter Street:

It was a very neighbourly place. People would mind children if mothers were ill, help with the washing and the cooking, that sort of thing. There were always lots of children from just born up to twenty-one. Being discharged at the end of your apprenticeship meant you had to go away. There were no jobs for skilled men in Swindon then other than the Works, so there were very few dependents over twenty-one in the village, perhaps a few young girls whose young men were away, waiting until they came home and married them when the girls were about twenty-three, twenty-four.

Ken Gibbs wrote later of the 1930s and '40s: 'We were a railway family, living in a railway street, in a railway area … and where just about every family had at least one member who worked

Women Steam Hammer Drivers, F1 & F2 Blacksmith Shop, outside the ladies' restroom, c.1949/50. From left to right, back row: Phil ?, Minnie Hacker, -?-, Vi Smith. Second row: Peggy Pedrick, Margaret Stone, Lorna Lawrence, Peggy Pinnegar, Nell Thorne. Third row: Emmie Thompson, Bet ?. Front: Pam Pinnegar who recalls:

> Our brother Ken worked as a blacksmith welder in F Shop. He told me they wanted girls in there and it was a man's wage. A girl on the hammer showed me what to do. The hammer I was taught off was just outside the offices. We were very young and didn't see any fear in the hammer. We just did it. We were about ten girls in there. We wore what we wanted but we had to go up the town and buy our own. Grace Varley and me just wore coat overalls. Some wore bib and braces. Some of the girls wore turbans. It was very fashionable then. It helped to keep their hair clean. No special shoes or anything like that. We had a rest room – through the Stamping Shop and out it was. We had one toilet, a sink and a place to hang our coats. We had a long table and a kettle.

'Inside'.' In fact seven out of the ten houses in his block housed families who worked in the Works. A similar pattern was repeated all along the street. Local folklore, passed down through the generations, tells the story of the unfortunate new, young teacher, an 'incomer' to the town. Trying to get to know his pupils better, he innocently asked one boy: 'Where does your father work?' 'Inside, Sir,' was the prompt reply. 'And mine Sir.' 'Mine too Sir,' the chorus went up. The poor man was overwhelmed. How could so many children proudly announce that their fathers were detained working 'inside' His Majesty's prisons?!

Family Connections

Working for the railway and for GWR was a family affair. Once the connection was established, sons joining their fathers, brothers, uncles, even grandfathers became the expectation. It was perfectly possible to be 'Inside' with one's granddad as the retirement age for those working 'Inside' was very 'flexible', particularly before the introduction of pensions, when the only alternative could be the dreaded Local Board Workhouse, so men worked until they were no longer physically able to. Petitions to the GWR Board for 'gratuities' give some idea of the situation:

October 1892

John Legg. Labourer. Rolling Mills Swindon.
Born 1818. Now 74 years old.
Worked with Engineers under Mr Brunel from 1835 to 1861 and various contractors in making portions of the GWR from 1861 to 1864.
Entered GWR service in Rail Mill 1864 – still on books. 28 years service.
Rate of Wages – 2/9 per day.
Has no private means and is blind with one eye, the sight of the other eye is also failing.

Robert Simpson. Brass finisher. Swindon.
Born 1814. Now in 78th year.
Entered Service October 1846 – 46 years.
Unable to work through illness.
Means – 5/6 per week.

To be retained to such an age these men had to be able to carry out some sort of useful work, as, although Works' Registers show the Company were often supportive of long-term men such as John Legg, the GWR also had a reputation of 'dropping men at the drop of a hat'. David Watson, a Scotsman from Aberdeen, was obviously a man who could work on! David served his apprenticeship and became a member of the Steam Engine Makers Society in Dundee in 1841. After working in Ireland and Dundee he walked to London in search of employment on the railways. Through the good offices of a friend he obtained an interview with Daniel Gooch and was taken on at Swindon Works where he worked for the next fifty years, not retiring until he was eighty! (Both his sons, Benjamin and David, followed him in and completed apprenticeships in the Works.)[16]

Another circumstance for staying on would have been any prevailing economic or critical situation at the time. During the 'Depression' years of the late 1920s and 1930s various measures were sought in order to reduce staff, sometimes in the least painful way. Circular 5236 dated 3 June 1931 advised that: 'it has been decided that the age for retirement of shop staff shall be reduced from 66 years to 65 years … and that the notice to be given of retirement reduced from three months to one month.' After the Second World War and even sometime after Nationalisation several thousands of men over sixty-five were still working. John Charlesworth remembers his granddad, Harry Garrett, nicknamed 'Smiler', was in there beyond 'normal' retirement age:

Granddad worked as a blacksmith in 14 Shop and would walk the six miles from Shaw to work every morning. During the war when he started at six, he had to be up at half-four. When I went in I used to go and see him sometimes. I can still see him sitting there with half

Rodney Charles Albert Butler, an electrician, seen working here on rewiring the rotor from a traction motor (sub-contracted work for Southern Region) *c*.1970. His grandfather, Charles, came down from London to Swindon Works in the 1880s. His dad, Clarence Horace but also known as Charles, spent his whole working life, apart from fighting in the First World War, in the C & W department as a coach body maker. His son Stuart worked briefly as a driver's mate on diesels in the 1970s, but is immensely proud of his Work's 'heritage' and has written several poems about it.

a loaf of bread and a kipper. That was his dinner. At sixty-five [in 1950 when there was still a shortage in skilled men] they'd given him the option to 'go on' and so he stayed, stayed until he was seventy! He retired in 1955.

Some families could count any number of family members working 'Inside' together over the years, and post-1874 this could also include daughters, widows and, later after the Second World War, even wives. The family of Ken Gibbs typifies this tradition:

My great-grandfather started with the GWR as a thirteen-year-old boy in 1849 working on plate laying/land drainage in the Didcot area. Family legend has it that in later years he was able to help the GWR establish, to their advantage, a boundary to certain properties, the reward for which was to have one son apprenticed to the premier trade in the Works as – fitter, turner and loco erector. This was to be my grandfather George, who started in 1875. Father, Sydney, followed on in 1909 ending up as Foreman in L2 and BB Shops. I started in 1944, also apprenticed as a fitter turner and loco erector, afterwards working my way through AM Shop, into Supervisory Staff & Management, CM&EE's Dept, then onto its Work Study Section. My Uncle Ernest was a crane examiner in G Shop. Uncle Charles worked in the Steam & Drop Hammer Shop. Father's two brothers, also apprenticed 'Inside', went at the turn of the nineteenth century to supervise railways in India. My wife Monica, and her sister, worked in GWR Accounts, her father George Kane was foreman in T Shop and her grandfather worked in the timber yard. Railway families all.

John Walter tells a similar story: 'I started my apprentice in fitting, turning and erecting in June 1945 and so joined my grandfathers Alfred and Fred, father John, uncles Stan, Vic, Bert, Fred, Harry, William and Wilf and numerous cousins'. Stuart Butler meanwhile writes in his poem 'Shopping in the Railway Works':

> I saw five generations of my family tramping through the tunnel,
> From village and from London,
> In search of work, wage and pride.

Eric Halliday's 'GWR tree' goes back to early GWR days when his great-grandfather, George, worked as an engine cleaner on the broad-gauge engines in Farringdon Engine Shed, whilst George's brother, Joseph, came to Swindon Works.

Relationship	Name	Date in Works	Occupation	Place
Great uncle	Joseph	unknown	unknown	Works
Grandfather	Richard Henry	1896-1925	carpenter	C & W
Father	Richard E. George	1911-1962	wagon builder	C & W
Uncle	Francis (Frank)	1913-1964	boiler-mate	Loco
Uncle	Herbert Reginald	1915-1966	wagon builder	C & W
Uncle	William Cyril OBE	1929-1978	metal machinist	C & W
★★	Eric	1942-1986	coach builder	C & W
Twin brother	Clifford	1942-1984	plumber	C & W
Sister	Elsie	1945-1952	clerk	Offices
–	Ernest Henry	1938-1985	carpenter	C & W
–	Hazel	1953-1960	clerk	Offices
–	Michael C.	1947-1980	clerk	C & W
–	Margaret	1984-1986	clerk	Offices

This amazing family record was disturbed only by military service.

Broad Gauge Loco *Aries* 2-4-0 Leo Class at Farringdon Engine Shed Berkshire, *c.*1865. Designed by Daniel Gooch, these were GWR's first goods engines. Eric Halliday's great-grandfather, George Halliday, engine cleaner, on the right, stands proudly in white trousers, holding an oilcan. Eric's family went on to have a long connection with the Works.

SWINDON WORKS' VETERANS INSPECTED BY THEIR MAJESTIES THE KING AND QUEEN, 28 APRIL 1924. EACH MAN HAD BEEN IN THE SERVICE OF THE GWR FOR OVER HALF A CENTURY.

Third row up, fourth from left, is Matthew Dickson, a fifty-two-year veteran.

The Dickson family also have a connection with the Works that lasted over 100 years. Andrew James Campbell Dickson, born 1833 in Fife, Scotland, travelled down to Swindon in the early 1860s with his wife Annie, young son Matthew and daughter Anne. His second son, George Wilson Dickson, was born in Swindon on 2 August 1868. Andrew, known to his family as 'an engineer', is actually identified on George Wilson's birth certificate as a 'factory engine driver'. Later on, however, on eldest son Matthew's marriage certificate of 1881, and on his own will, Andrew's occupation is then identified as 'railway clerk'. Whether Andrew had to give up work as an 'engine driver' because of an accident is not actually known but it is a probable explanation. Records show that the GWR often found light work for long service, infirm or disabled firemen and engine drivers.

Young Matthew Dickson started a six-year apprenticeship in January 1872 in the still quite new Carriage and Wagon Works, to 'learn the art of Carriage Finishing', one of the 'elite' trades. For Matthew it would have felt like 'a brave new world' with the promise of a secure and financially respectable future as a railway tradesman. In 1924 when King George V and Queen Mary visited the Works, an historical photograph was taken and Matthew, then aged sixty-seven but looking amazingly spry, wearing a trilby denoting his rank of either chargeman or maybe under-foreman, is in it. He had then clocked up an amazing fifty-two years of service. He remained 'Inside' for his whole working life until his retirement in the late 1920s.

Company records show George Wilson took up a six-year apprenticeship as an 'erector' in 1863 and finished his apprenticeship on 29 October 1889; thereafter he worked as a fitter on the Loco-side. George Wilson married Fanny, daughter of Ellen and Opie Smith, a boilermaker.

Their son George, known as Georgie, born 28 February 1912, reluctantly followed his father 'Inside' in 1927. Georgie had passionately wanted to be an electrician and work with radios, instead he took up a five-and-a-half-year apprenticeship in 'fitting, turning & erecting' which he hated. After the Second World War, on his release from war work at Wroughton Airfield, he returned to the Works and became a 'locksmith'. This work took him all over the site and into all the different workshops, so, unlike the majority of the workforce, he was able to freely wander the factory without hassle. In the reorganisation of the 1960s Georgie was transferred to work on gauges that came in for repair. In 1970, in recognition of forty years of service, Georgie received from BR a Long Service Award of a pair of binoculars (which he chose from the special Long Service catalogue also offering clocks, watches, teasmaids, or canteen of cutlery) at a presentation in the Works Dining Hall, By then, however, Georgie could see that it was the beginning of the end and urged his son Keith not to consider going into the Works, but seek alternative employment. He was right, as in 1973 he was offered retirement under the Redundancy Scheme which, being in poorly health, he took. Interestingly the letter he received telling him about the arrangements for his benefits and pension came from the 'Great Western Railway, Locomotive & Carriage Department, Sick Fund Society, Financial Accountants Office, British Rail Engineering Ltd., Swindon.' Sadly Georgie was undergoing tests for 'the Swindon Disease' when he died in 1987. His family believe that working with the asbestos inside the boilers was the reason behind this and the poorly health that had troubled him for many years.

Matthew had a large family, two daughters and five sons – George Campbell, William Edwin Frederick, Herbert, Sidney Gavin, and Frank, all born in Swindon. Matthew's first son, George Campbell, born 13 August 1882, followed his grandfather into the offices. After some years he was transferred to GWR's Reading office remaining for several years before being transferred back to Swindon in 1934. Here he rose through the ranks to a senior position in the Stores department and he is often mentioned in the *Great Western Railway Magazine* attending or presiding at events connected with the C & W Stores. He eventually became general storekeeper at Swindon, a position he held for the final eleven of a forty-seven-year career. The *Magazine* commented at his retirement in 1945 that: 'he had been an able officer and an amiable friend.'

William, born 29 January 1888, and Sidney Gavin, born 9 December 1898, both followed their father into the Carriage Department. William did a six-and-a-half-year apprenticeship in Coach Body Making, finishing on 28 January 1909, at which time, as with most apprentices, he was 'let go'. He took up employment with Daimler Cars at Coventry but in 1912 he took the boat to Australia to work for yet another railway company.

Sidney started his apprenticeship in 1912 just as his elder brother was emigrating. He must have wondered what *his* future would hold a few years down the line, little suspecting that the Great War was just around the corner which would change lives and history. Sidney joined the 'New Works' section of No.7 Shop where 250 men were then employed. In May 1918 he went into the RAF, which must have been very exciting for a young man from Swindon, swapping trains for planes! After his discharge in December 1919 he returned again to work in No.7 Shop. Forty-two years later in 1961 Sidney appeared alongside other craftsmen in a feature on the Works in the *Swindon Advertiser* telling of his work experiences and how conditions had happily improved. The number of men then in his shop had increased to 300. Sidney retired in 1963 having achieved over a half-century of service in No.7 Shop.

Matthew's youngest son, Frank, born 1901, was a bright lad who went to the local grammar school and then into the Works' Drawing Office as an apprentice draughtsman. He was not to stay and sometime after he completed his apprenticeship he moved to the railway at Birmingham, and later to the London Underground Acton Office.

Of the other brother, Herbert, it is not known for sure whether he actually worked 'Inside' but the family suspect that he may have worked in the Laboratory for a short time.

All the men who worked on the last steam locomotive to be built in the Works (and for British Rail) were proud to have done so, glad to have had a role in that iconic part of the Works and railway history. Driver Fred Simpson had a very special role as he took 92220 out for trials in its 'black coat'. Only after it had passed was it then returned to shop, painted green and its copper-top and nameplate *Evening Star* put on, before being finally 'outshopped' on 18 March 1960, when this splendid photograph was taken.

George 'Georgie' Dickson, seen in his usual dickie-bow tie, front first left, hated his apprenticeship so much so that he was known to curse his father when made to go inside the small confines of the boilers such as in 92220. As Georgie was inclined to claustrophobia this was bad enough, but that he also had to scrape their insides clean of the horrible filth and grime made him mad. He would loudly mutter how he wished he could rub his dad's face in it! This would often get him into trouble back home, as word of such mutterings would get back to his father. He did, however, enjoy his time as a 'locksmith', as, with the GWR's maxim of 'always repair, never replace' seeming to continue long after privatisation, he had many interesting challenges in keeping fixtures going, although 'everything had to be done just right, no matter what – no shortcuts, even if it was not the most economical way to do things'.

The first of the fourth generation in this railway family was George Kenneth, born 19 March 1913. He joined the GWR on leaving Swindon Technical College, and worked for sometime in the Laboratory before leaving and eventually becoming a senior chemist with the Atomic Energy Authority. Last in line and the last of the Dicksons to work 'Inside' is Ernest Gavin, born 15 October 1928, son of Sidney and great-grandson of Andrew. Ernest started in January 1944 while the Works was still GWR and while the country was again at war. He started as an office boy in the C & W 15 Shop office before moving on to the Staff Office and then the Cost Office. He was called up to serve in the RAF in 1947 and on his return to the Works two years later Ernest discovered that major changes had taken place – the Works was no longer part of the GWR, but was now British Rail. Ernest then worked in the Motive Power Department Staff Office, Western Region, until he was transferred to the Accountant's Department at British Railways Board HQ at Marylebone in March 1964, and so ended the Dickson's ties with Swindon Works.

The Dickson family served the GWR/BR at Swindon Works well down through the generations and the Works, it has to be said, served the Dickson family well too. When not giving them employment for their whole working lives, it had given them knowledge and transferable skills and a sound reputation that enabled them to have good employment possibilities and to progress well in their later careers.

Such a situation was common and many hundreds of other families could write similar work family histories even up to the closure of the Works in 1986. Such close ties helped strengthen both work-relationship bonds as well as personal friendships and developed that sense of belonging that almost everyone spoken to still fondly recalls, of belonging to 'one big railway family'. Arthur Jell tells how he became part of that 'big Works family' after demob in 1945:

> I went to the Labour Exchange. I said, 'Are there any jobs going in the factory, Inside, like.' He said, 'What do you want to do in there, then?' I said, 'Anything.' When I got in there I thought this will do me for a fortnight to see how it was, but I ended up spending thirty-eight years in there. It wasn't the money, because that wasn't very good. It was because of the attitude in there. Just a factory, but it was like a family. I enjoyed going to work. Once you went in there, you were in there life. I was sixty-four plus when I finished. I used to say I was 'Inside'. It's always a joke.

This sense of belonging, of being in one's 'right place' kept men in the Works, despite the poor conditions and often poor pay, and for those unfortunate enough to be 'let go', kept them coming back whenever an opportunity presented itself.

Once he'd finished his apprenticeship, Harry Murgatroyd, like many other apprentices, went to work as a journeyman in another company. He also, like lots of the Works engineering apprentices, did some 'turns' in the Merchant Navy and then joined a firm in Dagenham that made motor-car bodies. If it hadn't been blown up by bombs during the Second World War he may well have stayed, instead, requiring another job, he wrote to three different engineering firms including Swindon Works. Three letters came back, all offering a place, and Harry chose Swindon. Some men were drawn back again and again. Alan Lambourn captures this feeling of being 'magnetised' when he writes:

Talk to any Swindon Works' man (or woman) and they will always tell of the camaraderie and friendship they found 'Inside'. 'I used to look forward to going in to work', is an oft repeated phrase in many interviews. This picture reflects that friendly relationship spoken of. T Brass Shop, Loco Works 1962. L to r Arthur Rowe, turner (on lathe), Terry Bew, fitter, Ron Adams, chargeman, -?-.

having already experienced two previous periods of employment in the Works, and having vowed never to darken those walls again, I decided I wasn't interested when rumours of mass recruitment began to circulate. However, I was drawn by some magnetic attraction to make enquiries in November 1977 … and it goes without saying that I did go back and enjoyed a wonderful reunion with former workmates who had also been out in the big wide world.

The Way We Were

This 'magnetic bond' built upon workshop relationships, and the sense of 'belonging' was enhanced and cemented by many mutual interests and experiences, e.g. being part of 'God's Wonderful Railway'; working in the same shop; being on such-a-gang; being members of the same groups such as 'the Institute', the Shop Fund, the Shop band or football team; and even marrying other railwaymen's daughters and becoming your colleagues' son or brother-in-law,

In both the GWR and BR eras, athletics clubs were popular and well supported. In 1923 the GWR
Athletics Association competed against athletes from the French railway companies in Paris.
Top left: Seth Bruton, coach finisher 15 shop. Seated, first left: G. Bond and, first right, Seth's brother
Harry Bruton, fitter/turner Loco side. Seth's sprinting ability was legendary in the Works. Even in
his later years he could beat the younger men in their race down the tunnel and be away before
the rush!

thereby extending your actual real railway family. On top of all this there were the shared
community events like Trip, the annual Works' holiday, and the 'Children's Fête', as well as
taking part together in the great many activities on offer, initially through the Institute as well
as the Temperance Union, which later became the Social and Education Society (1923) and
finally in 1937 the very active Staff Association.

Despite their long working day and their long working week, and despite their hard,
physical toil, the men (and women) of the Works relished their free time and its opportunities
for play and recreation, These activities were a passport to another world, away from the
grime and grind of their everyday life. They not only brought a sense of freedom and self-
expression, but also gave one opportunities to do things, go places and meet people that one
would not have otherwise been able to do. A good example of this is in respect of athletics,
always popular and well supported, which took ordinary journeymen to exotic places like
Paris and Leipzig!

In 1960 the *Swindon Railway News* ran a small article highlighting what was on offer by the Staff Association for the amazing sum of 'FOURPENCE' – even in 1960 you didn't get much for that! Examples it gives are a packet of crisps (a good bit cheaper than today!), a bus fare (same again) and a couple of boxes of matches – for what it says is on offer that seems a bargain price. Not only is there still the use of 'the Mechanics' where its two choirs and dramatic section are very active, there is its famous library and reading room and a 'new spacious modern lounge where one can indulge in "indoor games" of darts, dominoes and skittles.' There is also the Shrivenham Road Sports Ground where one can participate in 'archery, athletics, bowls, cricket, football, hockey, tennis, putting and use the .22 rifle range and afterwards sit and relax at the bar.' All this had been built up from the original handful of workmen's interests in literature, music, drama and sports.

Through such groups and through their own talents a number of Works' individuals emerged to become known names in their times. In 1888 the local paper carried an article headlined: 'A SWINDON ATHLETIC HERO – A CHAT WITH KIBBLEWHITE'. It starts by stating: 'In Swindon at any rate, there is no need to ask "who is Kibblewhite?" His name is familiar in the mouths of all who are interested in athletics.' It goes on to say that indeed so familiar is Kibblewhite that he is known, like many celebrities today, by just his first name – 'Jimmy'. Such was Jimmy's fame that the paper tells how 'thousands would line the streets' if he was competing in a local road race. Sadly this hero of Swindon and Swindon Works is little known today so we may need to ask who was 'Jimmy' Kibblewhite?

James 'Jimmy' Kibblewhite (1866–1941) worked as a machinist in R Shop. He hailed from Purton and folklore suggests that he ran in from there to the Works each day, sometimes pitting himself against the workmen's train (known as Zulu) although, sadly, there is no firm evidence to support this! The *Advertiser* tells that: 'He stood just five foot nine inches, was wiry rather than massive of build' and without 'conceit or swagger'. He had a competence in more than just running, as he spent forty of his fifty working years as a chargeman.

Bob Townsend, who worked in T Shop and ran in BR's Railway International Team in the 1960s, is a big fan of Jimmy's and believes that Jimmy's workmates were too. Bob says: 'that Jimmy was held in high regard is borne out by the fact that immediately prior to his first attempt at an English title, an AAA Championship in 1889, his colleagues set up a subscription to enable Jimmy and his trainer to go to Weston-super-Mare for a fortnight to train.' It obviously paid off as Jimmy won! The GWR must also have been supportive as this was the time of unpaid holidays which were only taken at the Christmas, Easter and Trip closures, and so the GWR would have had to give special permission to Jimmy if such absence occurred outside these times. Most of the time his preparation and racing was sandwiched in between his full workday commitments:

I always, as a rule, work up to the night before the day on which I'm going to run, and sometimes I work on the day itself. You understand I don't give up work to prepare myself. My training is just this … I don't mortify the flesh in any way of diet. I take a spin when I get home after work of perhaps a quarter of a mile, or half a mile or three quarters; it depends upon the length of race in which I am going to run, but I never run the whole distance … I seldom drink anything, but when I do, it's a drop of Sherry during the time that I am what you may call training.

Jimmy Kibblewhite amassed many prizes and trophies for his running, which were exhibited in *The Mechanics* in 1888. He listed them as:

> All sorts and kinds – the usual description for prizes to amateurs … there are eight silver cups … a couple of tea and coffee services, cases of table cutlery and plated goods, half a dozen marble clocks, inkstands, cruet sets and a fine musical box. I have ten gold and silver watches and jewellery in quantities…. My medals number half-a-dozen – gold, silver and bronze.

The list of Jimmy's running achievements is spectacular. Not only was he a winner in cross-country as well as a flat runner, he was also a record breaker and world record holder. Some of his more notable achievements are:

1888 & 89	won Half-Mile Championship of Wiltshire.
1889	won One-Mile Championship of England.
1889	broke Three-Mile English & World Record in London.
1890	won One-Mile & Four-Mile Championship, also One-Mile Scratch Race and One-Mile Handicapped against 150 competitors all on the same day.
1891	won the English Country Championship.
1892	won Four-Mile Championship of England.
1892	broke Four-Mile Scottish Record at Glasgow.

Jimmy's retirement from the Works in 1930 was noted in the *Swindon Advertiser* as was his death in 1941, when they wrote calling him a 'Famous Runner of Former Days … a man who has achieved a certain greatness by his own efforts.'[17]

Unlike Jimmy before him, or artist Hubert Cook after him, Alfred Williams, poet, writer, linguist, now fêted as Swindon's own 'Hammer-man' was not celebrated nor readily appreciated during his time within the Works. Williams, at one time infamous in Swindon and in GWR circles for his book *Life in a Railway Factory* (1915), was a railwayman with rare literary skill, a discerning intellect and profound sociological insight, who had a deep sense of the injustice prevalent in the capitalistic world of the railways. He lived in South Marston, a small agricultural village several miles from New Swindon and walked or cycled to and from work each day. He was a man of amazing stamina and strong determination always seeking to broaden his mind particularly in respect of his passion for nature and folk customs. He wrote his books after each hard day's labour. He spent long hours studying and taught himself classic languages,

Alfred Williams wrote many books about rural folklore and customs but it was his book *Life in A Railway Factory* (1915) for which he is most remembered. This social commentary on the grim reality of life 'Inside' caused great bitterness and resentment against him at the time of its publication.

Hubert Cook, 'The Swindon Artist' known as Holly to his friends, worked as a machinist in the Boiler Shop for twenty-three years from 1916 to 1944. He studied art at evening class for many years at Swindon College. He constantly won the top awards at the Staff Association's Arts & Crafts Exhibition and in 1934 was presented with his prizes by the Head of the L.C.C. School of Arts & Crafts whose interest, with the Company's help of a free pass and one day paid absence, led to Hubert receiving a part-time scholarship from the Swindon Education committee to study at the Central School London, for four years after which he returned to full-time work in the Machine Shop. Some of Hubert's best-known works are lithographs of scenes inspired by his time in the workshops, one of which – 'Welder in the Boiler Shop' – was exhibited at the Royal Academy in 1943. Others have been exhibited all over the world in major cities such as Moscow and New York. Sadly, nowadays, few know of his name or of his talent.

even during working hours, often writing 'reminders' in chalk on his hammer. This practice ended as a clash of wills between 'those in charge' and himself, 'they' not just wiping them out but greasing the hammer to prevent him rewriting. Acknowledged as a good worker and tradesman he worked for many years as a 'hands-on' chargeman alongside his men, refusing promotion to foreman, not wishing to be 'over others'. Latterly his health paid the price for those long hours working over the smoke of his anvil and then hours of study. Forced to leave the Works because of ill health, he struggled to make ends meet for the years before his death, often relying on the goodwill of others, like his friend and admirer, and renowned Swindon Mayor, Reuben George, to assist in desperate times. His railway book, with its directness of style, makes compulsive reading, offering incredible, almost photographic cameos of the gritty, grinding reality of the working lives of the men and boys of his time is now accepted as a work of renowned stature.

Ken White is probably the best known locally, even internationally, of Swindon's contemporary artists. He is known for his famous murals all over the world, for his connection with Richard Branson, but especially for his paintings depicting life in Swindon Works and railway town, which is highly appropriate as it was the scenes he saw whilst working 'Inside' that inspired many of his iconic works. Ken followed his grandfather and his elder brother, Mike, 'Inside' in 1958. Starting as a rivet-hotter on a riveting gang, which he hated but which became the focus of many of his later paintings, he then happily transferred to sign-writing, the first apprentice for many years! Ken continued to study art at evening classes and eventually left the Works to study full-time. Since then he has earned his living by his palette and paintbrush. ('Signwriters' painting by Ken White)

Tough Times

The good times and good experiences nourished the 'Insiders'' community spirit, which was then tempered and strengthened by pulling together through the bad times and there were many of those down through the decades. In the difficult late 1840s this small railway community had faced unemployment and illness but by pulling together had brought about the wonder of the Medical Fund and saved New Swindon from disappearing off the map. Through the 1870/80s and even into the '90s another 'Great Depression' hit the country with heavy and sustained general unemployment and widespread gloom in the business world, yet Swindon again weathered the storm, even when the Company was laying off men elsewhere on the system. The rise and expansion of Swindon Works during this period is extraordinary. D.E.C. Eversley explores why this was so in his article 'The Great Western Railway and the Swindon Works in the Great Depression' (*Historical Journal* 1957). He gives a number of interesting explanations as to why the Works, in 'a one industry town', that could so easily have seriously floundered and even been 'killed off' for economic expediency by its own board, did so well against the trend over such a long period of time (1873–1896) during what he calls 'essentially a crisis of confidence'. Undoubtedly having the new Carriage & Wagon (from 1865) department sited alongside the Loco Works helped, but the reason he suggests that was the most significant for the Works, and one which I wholeheartedly support, is 'the position of the chief engineer', i.e. the Locomotive (later also Carriage & Wagon) Superintendent. (Later still in 1916 this position was given the title of Chief Mechanical Engineer and George Jackson Churchward was the

'SWINDON TOWN · F.C. 1923-4·'
ARCHER · DAWE · O'NEIL · NASH · RANDLE · WESTON · BENTLEY · GREEVES
COOPER·MASON DICKINSON·ROGERS , BEW· ING · POPPETT · RIDDLES)IN · WILKINS
DENYER ·CROSSLEY·PHILLIPSON· WAREING · JOHNSON· DANIELS ·THOMPSON · DAVIES

Swindon Town Football Club and Swindon Town football players hold a special place in Swindonians hearts. Jack Ing (middle row, fourth from left) came down from Windsor in 1913 and signed as a full professional footballer to Swindon Town. He played for two years and then war came and all football stopped. Jack went into the Works in 24 Shop as a painter. After the war he played part-time for the Town again, playing mostly right-half, but he spent the rest of his working days in 24 Shop. Part-time or not, Jack obviously made a lasting impression at the Club as they reported his death in very warm terms in their official programme (1974–1975).

News and Views · continued

Our older supporters will recall the one and only Jack Ing, who played seventeen seasons for Swindon between the wars.

Mainly a part-time player who never really commanded a permanent place in the First Team. No club ever had a more loyal servant and hard working player. He gave everything. Jack was always ready and willing to play anywhere, and at anytime. I can recall him scoring from the outside right position in the First Team, and the next week turning out in goal for the Reserve Team.

What a character! — the life and soul of the party. His presence lifted any team in the doldrums. He really was worth playing, if only for his effect on the team. He died on Sunday 23rd March, 1975 at the age of 89 years, a fine man, a splendid husband and father.

The club extends to his widow and children its deepest sympathy.

first.) The GWR were fortunate in their run of Works' superintendents. Gooch, 'the prototype of a new man' Eversley claims, led the way in 'the beginnings of the rule of the technocrat and "Managerial Revolution" of the twentieth century'. He was followed by Armstrong, a man of deep personal integrity, a Company man who looked after the Company's interest whilst also paying personal attention to the welfare of his men, so much so it affected his own health, whilst William Dean bore the brunt of these troubled times and is most remembered for being the one who had to contend with the difficulties of the Broad Gauge conversion and for being at the helm when, in 1882, the Works produced one new engine a week, one new coach every day and one new wagon every hour. It was an admirable record. Dean was followed by Churchward, his assistant through those last troublesome years. 'These engineers were men who held their posts through the strength of their professional qualifications and their character', says Eversley. They were also men who held the wellbeing of New Swindon very close to their hearts, taking an active part in the civic, educational and welfare side of the town's activities, working in co-operation with the men, and it is this, undoubtedly, that helped Swindon's fortunes and shaped its destiny, building strong community ties. I would add to Eversley's list their famous lieutenants, namely Archibald Sturrock, Minard Christian Rea, and Samuel Carlton, officers who not only worked 'Inside' but lived and socialised amongst the men too, helping build the social structures that bound them all together.

In 1900 'Old' and 'New' became just 'Swindon'. In 1901 when the Borough's new arms were granted, its railway heritage and presence was recognised by a winged engine-wheel and Locomotive No.3029 *White Horse*, which had been built in the Works in 1891. Population numbers then stood at just over 45,000. In 1908 the community's social resources were seriously called upon again. Cruelly, just before Trip holiday, significant numbers of men had been put on short time and then were laid off over the summer months so, by October, the distress in the town was dire. The local papers carried frequent articles about the deepening crisis, with headlines going from 'SHORT TIME AT THE G.W.R. WORKS SWINDON' in July to 'THE DISTRESS IN SWINDON' in October. In July G.K. Mills, Secretary of the Company, writing to the Revd. Canon Estcourt, Vicar of Swindon, as reported in the GWR's *Magazine*, defended the situation:

> The Directors deeply regret the necessity for the step [the large reduction of hands] ... but felt
> that in the circumstances they have no alternative. It is, of course, an incident of employment
> in all factories ... that workmen are taken on when busy and dispensed with when not. This,
> no doubt, must necessitate inconvenience, if nothing more serious, to those who lose their
> employment, but it is an inevitable feature of all manufacturing operations.

The *Advertiser*, seeking, perhaps, to reassure its readers, broached the subject from the premise that: 'the town is not being hurt by the discharges of men to the extent that it may appear on the surface ... rather it is has been the exceptional growth of work in the past two years, but that now there is to be some retrenchment.' In September the worsening situation had prompted the *Advertiser* to send a number of questions for the Company to respond to and Churchward, picking up on the paper's approach, answered in the best light he possibly could, stating: 'The number of men now employed after deducting all those recently discharged is 12,095, which compares with 12,250, in June 1904, 12,957 in June 1905, 13,323 in June 1906'. He admitted that although:'discharges have been made from time to time in the past years in considerable numbers … we have probably not reduced so many in so short a period'. Indeed, 1,228 is a significant body of men to be laid off. Churchward goes on to point out that the Company were being as helpful as possible, issuing passes to men to 'enable them to endeavour to find work and already they have issued 225 to men leaving the town for other places.' So great had the distress become that the Mayor, William H. Stanier, Stores Superintendent at the Works, proposed the setting up of a relief fund. Donations and weekly subscriptions were made by all sectors of the town as well as from the numerous Works' Societies. The large families of the registered unemployed were a source of great concern, so the Education Committee made arrangements to feed 'necessitous children' at school with the help of the Fund. This is an amazing example of a community looking after its own. Here one can see not just anecdotal evidence but tangible proof of the strong kindred spirit and kinship that existed amongst the people of this railway town. Such kinship was shown yet again in the well known 'Great Depression' of the 1930s, although it hit Swindon as early as the late 1920s. For those at the Works it resulted in many periods of short-time working and layoffs – 800 notices were served on one Friday, 30 September 1932. It was called 'a Black Weekend' and long remembered as such. 'The Swindon Council of Social Service to relieve poverty, distress or sickness' was set up. It established a clothing depot,

From left to right: Eric Halliday, coach builder, later worked as an estimator and then on Work Study, father Francis, 'Frank', wagon builder, and Eric's twin brother Clifford, plumber, all worked on the C & W side. Eric started in the Works aged fourteen in 1942 during the Second World War. In his first week he turned up for work after an air raid to find 'the end of 13 Shop had disappeared, blown away by the bomb'. When he was just fifteen Eric was told he had to join the Home Guard, which his dad was in, or the Cadets, so he joined the Air Training Corps, training at weekends. He was also involved in Fire Watching. On top of all this, as an apprentice Eric had to do two nights a week at night school – all after a hard day's work.

allotments and a pig farm, boot and shoe repair classes, and grocery and other grants were made from its assistance fund. Jack Harber recalls the 'Farthing Buffet' organised and run by the Swindon Women's Free-church Council, but generously supported by local grocers, the Co-op and railwaymen from their allotments. Jack writes in his memoirs:

> The idea was to charge a farthing [a quarter of an old penny] for each item. Thus a round of sandwiches, usually ham or cheese, cost one farthing; a generous slice of pie was a farthing, a cup of tea was a farthing. So, for three-farthings a man could get a good meal and leave money to feed his family – unfortunately wives and families could not be catered for due to the lack of funds.

It was at times such as these that the 'Insiders' were pleased to belong to the Institute, the Sick Fund Society and the Medical Fund, although when men left the Company, they automatically ceased to be members of the latter.

The two world war periods were other critical times when community spirit and resolve were put to the test. The Second World War saw the emergence of a new 'working gang', a new 'band of brothers' – the GWR's own Home Guard.

GWR Swindon Battalion of the Home Guard march alongside the J1 Iron Foundry inside the Works, 1941.

Above: During the Second World War many railwaymen were in 'protected trades', prohibiting them from joining the Forces. Instead, men in the Works joined 'the Local Defence Volunteers' which became 'the Home Guard' on 23 July 1940. Originally '3 Company' in the 5th Battalion Wiltshire HG, the 13th Battalion (GWR) Home Guard was inaugurated, under Lt-Col. Dyer, on 1 May 1943. Consisting of seventeen officers and 623 other ranks it eventually had five full Companies. They would put in the hours after their arduous day's (or night's) work. Their 'command station' was located at 3 Emlyn Square, although they answered to Salisbury Plain District HQ, and there was a rifle range in the Works' Laboratory where practises were held. In 1944 they set up camp at Lydiard Park for a three-week-long intensive exercise. Training began with lectures and demonstrations leading on to bayonet drill, map reading, camouflage instruction, night movements and battle drill. Operations were co-ordinated by wireless and walkie-talkie and live ammunition was used to ensure realistic battle conditions. Here they assemble 'On Parade' outside the Carriage Finishing Shop.

Opposite below: Swindon Works Members of the 13th Battalion, GWR (Wiltshire) Home Guard. From left to right, front row: Mr F. Raven, Foreman AW Shop. Mr E. Chegwidden, CMEE Offices. Mr R. Fricker. Mr M. Tucker, Workshops. Dr Bennett (Park House). Captain J. Haynes, Regular Army. Lt-Col. S.A.D. Dyer, 16 Office CMEE. Captain T. Tarry, Quarter Master, Regular Army. Captain Morse, Workshops. -?-. -?-. Mr Miller, 38 CMEE Office. Photo taken outside of 9 Shop Carriage Trimming, Carriage & Wagon Works, c.1944.

Arthur 'Art' Townsend was a boilermaker by trade but worked as warehouse staff in Timber stores between 1941 and the 1950s. He kept a journal of his Home Guard commitments. These small abbreviated extracts give us some idea of what was involved:

1941
JANUARY

THR 2 -   Air Raid warning 7.30pm. All Clear
           12.10am. Bed early for H.G Duty
FRI 3 -   H.G. Duty 1.15am – 5am. Air Raid
           warning 11.30pm All Clear 6.15am
           Sat.
SAT 4 -   Air Raid Warning 6.55. All Clear
           8 pm. A.R.W. 10.40pm. All Clear 7am
           Sun
SUN 5 -   H.G. Parade
TUES 7 -   7.45 Evelyn Sq. Lecture on H.G.
           Cyclist Duty Action Stations
WED 8 -   H.G. Lecture on Gas Mask and
           Gasses at Platoon H.Q A.R.Warning
           3.15pm. All Clear 3.30
THR 9 -   A.R.W 9.30pm A.C 5am Fri.
SUN 12 -   H.G. Parade Drill (morning)
           H.G. Duty 9.30 – 1.15am GWR
           Transfer
WED 15 -   H.G. Lecture on Lewis Gun

1942
AUGUST

SUN 16 -   H.G. Parade
MON 17 -   Bombs dropped (Kembrey Street)
           11.30pm. House damaged. Front roof
           off
TUES 18 - Clearing up Air Raid damage all day
TUES 25 - H/G Duty 10.00 – 5 am GWR
WED 26 -   H/G Parade

SAT 29 -   Bombs dropped in Drove Rd 9.00am
SUN 30 -   H/G Parade

SEPTEMBER

THR 10 -   Attended Ambulance class GW
           Station
SAT 12 -   Reported for duty 7.30pm. Invasion
           practice started 5.30pm
SUN 13 -   H/G Invasion practice finished
           1.30pm

1943
FEBRUARY

MON 1 -   H/G NCO Instructions Meeting
TUES 2 -   H.G. duty 10.00pm – 6am GW
           Works
WED 3 -   H.G. Parade No 3 PLAT. H.Q in 4
           Shop
MON 8 -   H.G. NCO Meeting Drill
           Instructions
WED 10 -   H.G. Parade in 4 Shop A.G
           Instructions
WED 17 -   H.G. Parade Firing Practice Rifle
           Range
WED 24 -   H.G. Lecture on Ammo

1944
DECEMBER

SUN 3 -   H.G. Parade. Finished, Took
           shelter down
SAT 9 -   Returned H.G. equipment

The famous 'Tunnel Entrance' in London Street that led from one world to another 'Inside'.

Name Change – GWR to BR

After Nationalisation, despite the loss of the GWR brand, the town still thought of itself as 'Great Western' and still definitely, first and foremost, a railway town with the Works at its heart. The simple change of initials from GWR to BR – British Rail – brought an emotional and cultural shock to the town. Through the next few decades, as British Rail underwent its various changes and more 'incomers' came to the town and to the Works, the notion of 'Insiders' still persisted and influenced people's lives, even in small, simple things that just said 'railway'. Arthur Jell gives an example of this:

> They would make the clothes lines in the Works. They would be boiler tubes – full length of the engine they were, and they would take them home on the corporation bus at night. They were all over Swindon. Still there now I expect. Joe Cook, he made his and took it on the bus. Just shoved it up the middle of the bus like. Nothing ever bothered that bloke, Joe Cook.

Swindon Works or 'Inside' has become a cultural phenomenon of Swindon and 'Insiders' a cultural identity. Undeniably Swindon Works' railwaymen and women were a close-knit community, one which, to quote Brian Maddicks: 'there is nothing in this society today to match and one that it is doubtful we shall ever see the like of again.'

Endnotes

1. Unacknowledged *The Town and Works of Swindon*, p.11.
2. Cattel & Faulkner, p.47.
3. Crittal et al (1983), PRO previous ref. HL 1/1/2.
4. Hudson, p.50.
5. Silto, p.43.
6. Crittal.
7. Platt, p.103.
8. Information taken from Eversley (1957).
9. Darwin, p.18.
10. Second World War female recruit.
11. Cockbill (1988), p.31.
12. Ibid, p.23.
13. Cockbill (1988).
14. The Town & Works of Swindon.
15. Francis Bevan, *The Swindon Advertiser*, March 2008.
16. Information provided by Bob Townsend.
17. Thanks to Bob Townsend and Mike Stubbs for information on Kibblewhite and use of article 'Wiltshire World Record Holders in the North Star' Vol. 9, No.4, autumn 2007.

CHAPTER 2

Controlling the Workers

It is an inexorable rule of nature that wherever there is a collection of people (gangs, teams, companies, unions, governments, to name but some) there will need to be someone, or some few, in control. It is also inevitable that those in control will need a variety of means to exert and enforce this control. The Industrial Revolution introduced vast numbers of manual workers into production systems and into systems of control previously not exercised on such a scale. 'In the big industrial enterprises which characterised the Industrial Revolution … they had to control the conditions of production to a degree never previously envisaged or attempted and they were ruthless in the methods they used in order to do this,' states Kenneth Hudson in his notable book *Working to Rule*, a study into railway discipline. The book is an exposition of the savagery of the way the working masses in a particular 'system', i.e. the railways, were kept under control. This approach was not, of course, confined just to the railways. Others had acted in such a way before them. For their internal organisation the railway companies took the military model and, just as in military service, they expected nothing less than total commitment, total loyalty and especially total obedience from their men. Just as military men were doing 'service' so were railwaymen (and women) expected to do 'their duty' and be loyal 'servants'. Just as the military was run by rules, so were the railways governed and run. There were several 'tools' the companies used to keep control; for the GWR these included the apprenticeship scheme, the 'Indenture' or Apprenticeship Agreement, the piece rate, time records and the clock, but especially and particularly 'the Notice', the Company Rules and Regulations, the foreman, and, in the case of Swindon Works, the tenancy of the Company houses, 'the check' and the 'hooter'. For the men at Swindon Works by far the most infamous was The Rule Book, by far the most feared was the Foreman.

The Company Houses

Even when they had left their place of work at the end of the day the early Works' workmen still felt the heavy hand of their employer as most of them lived in the Company's houses. From the beginning the Company exerted control over the water provision and gas provision to

The provision of the 'Company 'ouses' as they were commonly known, often viewed as a paternalistic gesture, was, in fact, a practical solution based on hard-edged economics to resolve a dire problem, i.e. no houses = no workers. The gracious-looking fronts of these 'one-up and one-down' cottages belied their 'backsies' or backways humble and basic reality. Edward Snell wrote in 1843: 'The Company make the men pay most extortionate rents for these bits of huts – 3s 6d for a single and 7s for a double cottage.'[1]

the villagers, punishing them if they left water taps open by restricting the supply to a limited time. The families knew that they could only remain tenants as long as 'the man of the house' worked 'Inside', and that any misdemeanour, whether in work or out, could result in being evicted. Dismissal notices show that one chap was dismissed for damaging the drinking cup on the water fountain in the Park. Works Manager William Gooch had a particularly troublesome time dealing with the tenants, writing to them again and again as in November 1859:

It has come to my knowledge that many of the boys of New Swindon are very unruly and mischievous in their conduct, especially during the evenings when property is frequently damaged and, as on a recent occasion, life endangered. Parents in most cases are to blame for not checking such bad conduct amongst their children.

I consider it my duty for the protection of the Inhabitants and the Company property and shall not hesitate to discharge any man who allows his family to continue to commit such offences.

Within the village the hierarchy of 'Inside' was still maintained so that officers and foremen got the bigger, better houses, a physical and visible sign of their status. The cottages in Faringdon Road, one of the last rows to be built, were bigger in size, having three bedrooms and two downstairs rooms. These were mostly occupied by foremen, so much so that it became known as 'Foremen's Road'.

Tenancy of the houses was always under pressure and the Company were constantly monitoring its tenants. In March 1895 William Dean was not happy to discover tenants who should not have been there. He writes in Circular No.926: 'In the event of a Company's servant who is a tenant of the Company's Houses, dying and leaving a widow or children occupying the house, the case must be reported to me. I find that in two cases children left without father or mother have been allowed to continue as tenants, which is quite contrary to the Company's regulations.' He follows this up in yet another circular with instructions that in future the 'Leaving Voucher' must be marked 'tenant' or 'non-tenant' presumably so that the Management can keep an even firmer control on the matter.

Even as late as 1926 the GWR exercised their control over the workers and what happened in the village on their land. Jack Harber remembers what happened during the General Strike:

I was ten years old in 1926 and lived in the railway estate. Most of the strike activities took place around the estate. The Strike meetings were held in the park and the picketing took place at the main entrance. As the estate and park were private property any strike activity was trespassing. W. Robins and W. Noble, who were Secretary RCA and District Secretary AEU, were arrested for trespassing during a picket.

This controlling influence through property relaxed when the GWR ceased to exist in 1948, when the tenancy came under the jurisdiction of British Rail. The houses were still reserved for railwaymen and women who worked 'Inside', but widows no longer need worry about being evicted when their husbands had died. Later from 1966 the houses were sold on to the Borough Council who opened up the tenancy to anyone on the Council's housing list, and the direct link to the Works was finally broken.

Tenant or not, so invasive was this 'outside' control over the workers that it pervaded all private and family lives. Alfred Williams highlighted this aspect of the hold of the Company over the men when he wrote:

… even at home in his private life and dealing, a man is under the eye of his employer … his liberty is tyrannically restricted. In town he is not allowed to supplement his earnings … he

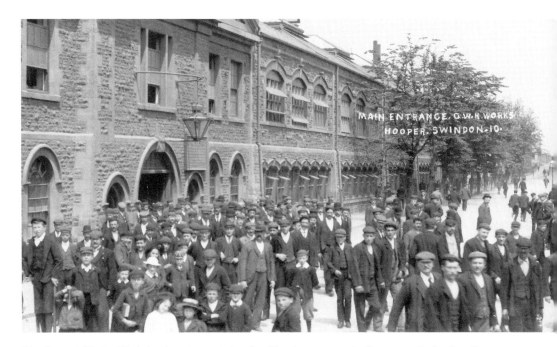

Standing outside the Works' main entrance in London Street some pose for the camera before heading off home, the workers knew that even when they had left the Works they had not left the Company's heavy hand behind them. 'Inside' and out, their lives were moulded by Company policy and practice. (Paul Williams' Hooper Collection)

may not even sell apples or gooseberries … it is the unprotected unskilled workman that most chiefly be terrorised or subjugated.

Indeed 'trading' was specifically against Company rules. Whilst Williams talks of outside trading, Hudson tells of 'Inside' trading when, in the first years of the nineteenth century, money-lending between 'financial specialists' and their fellow workers was active. In later years inside 'trading' could also include 'the tuck-shop-drawer' from where a workman would sell goodies to hungry staff. Roy Taylor remembers in the 1940s there was one chap in K Shop who would take orders to bring in lardy cakes from Wootton Bassett, but this was put a stop to by the foreman. In the difficult 1930s so much 'trading' was going on in respect of tobacco, cigarettes and even tea, that in June 1932 the General Manager issued instructions and C.B. Collett passed them onto the Works that no such activity must be undertaken 'by any members of the Staff on the Company's premises or in the Company's time'. In the 'swinging sixties' one clerical gentleman had a drawer full of 'something-for-the-weekend' for those men who couldn't get to the barbers or chemist. Over the decades it was always known that there were 'bookie's runners' in a number of shops. In F Shop it was the shop office clerk. There was a ritual. The punter would approach Arthur with a nod of the head. Arthur would lift the lid of his sloping desk and the bet would be slipped inside. Later Arthur would slip out and place all the bets and, later still, go back for the winnings; obviously there had to be an understanding with the watchmen on the gate. In the 1960s this 'running' began to get out of hand, with so much time dedicated to it that verbal warnings went down the chain of command to bring it back to 'acceptable' levels that the foreman could turn a blind eye to. Even in the 1980s just before closure, one man was 'trading' as a barber and would offer cheap cuts on a Friday afternoon in the boilershop behind a screened-off tender parked up in the corner. So popular was this particular 'trading' it is remembered that the ground around was always a foot deep in hair cuttings!

The Notice

Probably the earliest internal method for levelling mass control where the Company 'spoke' to and directed the men was through the use of 'the Notice', either sent directly to the Contractors and Foremen for them to implement and enforce, or posted on the Works' gates and put out in general to the workmen. These would come from the Works Manager and/or his assistant. In August 1854 the Works Manager, Minard Christian Rea, had cause to write an intriguing notice:

> **Notice to the Workmen Employed at the Swindon Works**
> Within the last few days several anonymous letters all in the same hand-writing have been addressed to different parties connected with these Works, myself among the number, some of the letters reflecting upon an Officer in the Company's service in the most scurrilous and obscene language, and one of them concerning two of your own body, obviously written with the intention of injuring them. Such a course I have always discouraged as it is destructive to the good feeling which should exist in such an Establishment as this and if sanctioned no man is safe. I do not offer any reward for the discovery of the author of these letters, but I have a strong reliance upon the proper feeling which I know exists among you, to have such infamous conduct exposed. I cannot produce some of the letters not feeling myself justified in exposing the names of unoffending parties in connection with infamous and obscene language, but I append to this the letter involving the character of your two fellow workmen to afford the opportunity of identifying the writing, in the full confidence that if the writer can be exposed he will be.

It is a fascinating piece of text in the way Rea − known to have worked tirelessly for the betterment of the workmen, in terms of their physical wellbeing and in 'civilising' them − tries for empathy and to engage the men's better natures in judgement over their fellow workmates.

'Notices' covered all manner of things, from giving of information to stern warnings. Examples of these are:

> **December 1856 Holiday Notice**
> Christmas day and New Year's day will be the only holidays at the approaching season.
> Application for Passes to be made to the respective foremen not later than Friday 19th inst., after which non can be granted.
> Signed John Fraser. [Assistant Manager]

> **February 1857 Notice to Workmen Snow Balling**
> Any person detected throwing Snow Balls into or about the entrance of the Works or within the Works will be discharged.

June 1858 Notice

Complaints having been made to me that workman pass through and remain about the Stores Yard during meal hours and that mischief is done by boys playing there, Notice is hereby given that any person reported to me as so doing will be heavily fined and if guilty of a second offence be discharged. No Person will at any time be allowed to enter the Stores Yard except those required there on duty.

Signed William Gooch, Manager.

Another intriguing 'Notice' of 2 November 1859 from W. Gooch declares: 'having observed a number of Workmen leave the Works at 6pm with hand lamps during the Winter months, I hereby give notice that in future no persons will be permitted to bring lamps into or take them out of the Works unless by my special authority.' He also sent a note to the Watchman, Mr Baker, to instruct him to inform 'the Policeman of the Works' to do this and report anyone found 'so doing'. Bearing in mind that this is November, and the men will be arriving and leaving work in the dark, many from surrounding villages, it seems overly harsh. If the Company were worried about fires they could have insisted that lamps were extinguished at the entrance or not lit until having left the Works. They did not need to ban them entirely.

C.B. Collett, who took up the post of Locomotive Works Manager in 1913, obviously wanted his Notices noticed as he issued this curt directive soon after:

In order to ensure that 'Notice' information was available and accessible to the workers, each shop eventually had its own notice board which Rule 8 of 1874 tells was 'nailed up on the shop doors'. Later notice boards were placed near the shop entrance to catch the men's early attention. 'The Notice' was used to censure, inform and instruct, and the variety of notices shown in this photograph, taken in B Shed on 26 June 1930, cover all those aspects. (David Hyde Collection)

October 1914 Obsolete Notices
Please have all Notices that are out of date or that have served their purpose including Army Notices removed from your notice boards and have the notice boards cleaned down and where necessary re-painted. This matter is important in order that fresh notices that are issued may be quickly and clearly seen.

Sometimes the 'Notice' seems to be a way for the managers to let off steam as in this fine example. So vexed is Collett in this instance that it is also all set in capital letters:

NOTICE TO MEN WORKING WITHIN SIGHT OF THE MAIN LINE
I REGRET TO LEARN THAT A NUMBER OF THE TRAVELLING PUBLIC AND MANY OF THE COMPANY'S OFFICIALS HAVE THE IMPRESSION THAT THE MEN EMPLOYED IN THESE WORKS ARE AN EXTREMELY SLACK LOT, AND THAT THEY HAVE NOTHING BETTER TO DO BUT LOLL ABOUT AND GAZE AT PASSING TRAINS.
I KNOW IT IS DIFFICULT TO AVOID LOOKING AT A TRAIN WHEN IT PASSES, BUT I SHALL BE GLAD IF YOU WILL ENDEAVOUR TO CORRECT THIS IMPRESSION IN FUTURE BY BEING BUSILY ENGAGED AT WORK AT SUCH TIMES.
Signed C B Collett.

'Larking' and 'idling' such as demonstrated here by Bob Townsend in T Shop during the 1960s, are remarked upon in official circulars over several decades. It brings to mind the popular and oft-told joke: 'How many men worked in the Works?' Answer: 'Half of them!'

The notion of men 'lolling', 'idling' or 'larking' had caused the GWR great annoyance from early times, so much so that it was incorporated into the Rules as shown in those of 1874. Rule 16 states: 'Anyone disturbing the order of the work by fighting or *larking* ... will be punished by fine or dismissal as the nature of the case may deserve.' Presumably the snowballing in 1857 was one such 'larking'. 'Idling' and even 'playing' were also in the revised version of rules in 1904 incurring a 2s 6d fine as well as those 'playing' being held responsible for the 'expenses to which the Company may be put' should such actions result in an accident.

Some Notices mark particularly iconic times in history, such as that posted out on 2 May 1926 by the general manager, Felix J.C. Pole, in relation to the 'General Strike'. Pole did not mince his words, which were direct and forceful:

NOTICE TO THE STAFF

I appeal to all of you to hesitate before you break your contracts of service to the old Company, before you inflict grave injury upon the Railway Industry, and before you arouse ill-feeling in the Railway service which will take years to remove.

Remember that your means of living and your personal interest are involved and that Great Western men are trusted to be loyal to the conditions of service in the same manner as they expect the Company to carry out their obligations and agreements.

Another was the one in 1940 notifying the men in the Works that Trip, the annual holiday, had to be cancelled because of the war! 'The Notice' was often the harbinger of bad news, especially when informing the men of 'short-time' working which happened so many times down the decades, especially in the 1920s and '30s. In the days when health and safety became more enforced, Notices would detail the dos and don'ts of such regulations and as the unions became more visible and active these would jostle for space alongside notices regarding union matters. 'The Notice' continued to be used throughout the years until the very end of the Works. In the 1960s, '70s, and finally '80s, BR notices were once more harbingers of doom and gloom as they carried information regarding impending redundancies and, finally, closure.

Employment and Apprenticeship

A more oblique way that control was exerted over the workforce was through the promise of employment for sons and, although on a much more limited scale, daughters and widows. This was of particular significance when Swindon was a 'one-industry' town. Boys who misbehaved put their future prospects in jeopardy as William Gooch brought emphatically, with underlining, to their attention in June 1869: 'Boys brought before my notice as committing such depredations [damage in the village] will not in the future <u>at any time </u>be employed in the Works.' This coveted prize, 'the apprenticeship', was a double-edged sword, both a promise and a burden; for Roy Blackford, who joined in 1943 it was the latter:

> I never wished to join the GWR. I had done very well at school and would liked to have continued my education, but an apprenticeship of £100 to those who had to pay, was too much for my parents to turn down, so I found myself facing two years of hard labour in a very noisy and dusty atmosphere, even before I could start my apprenticeship.

It is said that GWR men came with GWR stamped on their bottoms, their destinies mapped before their birth even and the same could also be said for those who worked 'Inside' even after Nationalisation. Most saw this as a good thing that led the way to becoming one of the 'aristocracy of skilled tradesmen' whose GWR/Swindon Works reputation could get them a job worldwide, but for a goodly number it was undoubtedly a curse. A curse because it led them to a preordained working life whose shape and fortune was largely outside their control, decided upon by others 'from above' and based on the 'status' level of their father's work. Frank Saunders explained:

> It was mapped out for you … people knew. The teacher would say, 'Where are you going to work?' 'Inside,' that's what you'd say, 'Inside the railway.' 'Right, what are you going to be?' 'Oh, I don't know, Sir.' 'Well, what's your father?' 'He's a machinist.' 'Well you can be a machinist.' Your father would go over to the Manager's Office or see the foreman and that would be it.

Try as they might, no matter how quick or academically bright they might be, the boys could not 'buck the system'. As Frank Saunders said: 'They had to knuckle-down and accept or seek their fortune elsewhere.' This was expected and accepted thinking but, however expected it was, many a young lad's hopes and dreams for other things were dashed by this excessive control.

Influence, it was also known, was one way round a lot of things, even in the matter of work assigned. Alfred Williams wrote bitterly of the role of 'influence' in his time, as did Hugh Freebury: 'I heard a lot about "influence" from the men in the workshops. It was understood, it was not *what* you knew but *who* you knew. It went on all the time, this keeping in with the right people.' John Attwell, talking of his time in the 1940s, frankly recalls: 'It was not easy for a premium apprentice to get in as a fitter. Fitting apprenticeships were the most prized and coach fitters were a class above. I got into the Finishing Shop for one reason – my father knew the foreman.' For those not 'in the know' it meant accepting what was given. Few dared challenge this order of things, knowing that if they did, their own and possibly their sons' jobs might be at risk.

The Freebury family on TRIP holiday. Harry Freebury, first left, a machineman on 40s a week in the 1930s, could not, despite his entreaties and his son Hugh's excellent school record, secure Hugh, third from left, an apprenticeship at his own trade because of this low rate. 'If you were on the top rate – 42s – we might consider it,' he was told, so, for the sake of 2s a week, Hugh was detailed to boilermaking, which he said 'carried the reputation of being more of a disease than a trade'. Harry, normally a retiring man, at his wife's and Hugh's insistence bravely returned to the Managers' office several times to try to change Hugh's fortunes but could never bring enough influence to bear to do so. Hugh eventually left the Works and enjoyed a career in academia.

One of the few who did dare brave the lions in their clerical den was a Mr Alfred Parker, a 'humble moulder in the J Shop or Iron Foundry'. His mighty stand is told by Hugh Freebury. Mr Parker was greatly upset that his son Ronald, a bright and intelligent lad, who had not only matriculated but did so with honours, the highest award obtainable, plus five distinctions, was only offered a workshop apprenticeship for fitter, turner and erector. Whilst, admittedly, the crème de la crème of trades and a good bit above his own station, it was not what Mr Parker had hoped for, for Ronald. He had hoped to see his lad become one of the '9 o'clock staff' in the hallowed main offices and so he resolutely refused the offer, sending Ronald off to train for management in 'an exclusive shoe shop in Old Town'. The story, however, did not end there. Having discovered that a boy who had only managed a 'General Schools' qualification, but was the son of a Mr Wainwright, a fitter, had been offered one of the coveted clerical posts, Mr Parker was so incensed he took himself back to the Managers' Office and demanded an explanation. This was not a situation that Mr Wetherall, the clerk in question, was used to. Freebury tells how: 'for once the dignified, imperturbable clerk was thrown off balance … muttering that several factors had been taken into consideration in the decision making.' 'Such as his father's a fitter and I'm only a moulder,' Mr Parker declared. This Mr Wetherall vehemently denied, suggesting rather that things such as loyalty, length of service and good service were what he meant. Alfred Parker challenged him yet again demanding whether this implied his service to the Company 'might not be all that it should'. Then Mr Parker delivered his Daniel-like *pièce de résistance*:

> Let me make myself quite clear, Mr Wetherall. If you're not able to offer my son at least a similar post to the one the other boy's got in the Boiler Shop, that is an office clerk's job, I'm going to take this further, right to the top if necessary, even if it costs me my own job. I hope I make myself quite clear because that's exactly where I'm leaving it at present, but I don't intend to be too patient on the matter.

It was a magnificent stand for a normally mild-mannered man but it paid dividends. In less than a week Ronald was requested to attend for a medical examination in Park House and then to report to L2 Shop as a junior clerk on the 8 a.m. staff. Thanks to his dad, Ronald was on his way to a probable 9 a.m. start![2]

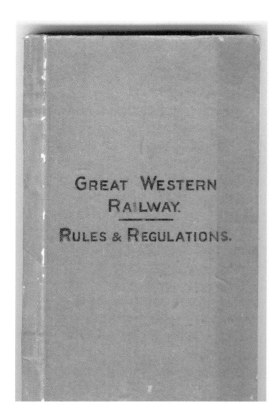

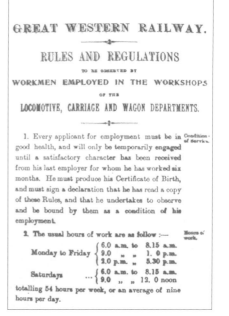

Rule Book of 1904. Rule No.3 to join the Medical Fund notes – *applies to Swindon Works only.*

The Rule Book

The infamous GWR Rule Book laid out the terms and regulations of the railwayman's working life. Each workman was given his own little book specific to 'the Workshops of the Locomotive, Carriage & Wagon Departments' which, upon entry to the Company, they had to sign to say they had 'carefully read (or had them read to me) [and] clearly understood them' and to signify their agreement to 'bind myself to observe and obey the foregoing Rules and Regulations.' It would appear that a long time before Mao, 'The Rule Book' was just as subjugating as his *Little Red Book*.

The rules, set up primarily for administration reasons as well as to control the workforce, were also there to minimise accidents, avoid physical disasters, prevent misuse or wastage of materials and assist production, although not necessarily in that order. The 1904 and 1916 'Rules and Regulations to be observed by the workmen employed in the Workshops of the Locomotive, Carriage and Wagon Departments' lists thirty-nine separate items. That of 1874 lists only twenty-four. Marked differences between them are a) 1874 has separate sections headed up 'Conditions of Employment', 'General Rules' and 'Particular Rules for Mechanics, Boiler Makers, Smiths etc.,' whilst 1904 and 1916 (and others thereafter) are not sectionalised; b) the 1874 rules attracting 'punishments' are banded together, whereas those in 1904 and 1916 are within the whole listing. The first handful of rules which deal with 'housekeeping' are basically the same throughout although the terminology is slightly different. These cover conditions of employment/service; hours of labour/work; notice to leave/resignation and dismissal; absence from work/duty; as well as addressing payment of wages; time tickets; time books; leaving or entering work; and leaving work without permission. In 1874 nine of the rules incur punitive fines to a maximum of 5*s*, whilst in 1904 one-third of the thirty-nine carry fines ranging from 6*d* up to 2*s* 6*d*. In 1874 five rules 'render himself liable to dismissal' while for 1904 it is *fifteen* — and its No.35 also carries '*and prosecution*'.

There are a great many rules regarding 'tools' as GWR were continually exercised by keeping control of these. Pilfering, losing or lax attention to returning items was a never-ending problem. In November 1853 Minard Rea had posted a staggering 'Five Pound Reward' for information leading to 'a conviction of person or persons' who had broken open several tool boxes in the Works and 'extracted the tools therefrom'. Tools such as hammers, taps, dies, rimers and chisels were provided by the Company and in November 1870 Samuel Carlton tried a new approach to keep tabs on these wandering items:

> I shall be glad if you would have all the Tool boxes in your shop numbered and the tools marked with the corresponding no., so that in the case of tools being lost or stolen we may be able to trace them. Also please keep a register showing the Nos. of boxes, the quantity of tools, and the names of the persons to whom they belong.

Later the workman had to ensure the issued tools carried the 'initials of the Company, as well as his own private mark' (this mark came to be his 'check' number). This custom then continued right through. The rule against 'breaking open drawers and boxes and using or taking other men's tools' is very understandable. Apart from wanton damage, having to make new tools was time wasting and costly as not only did it involve the cost of the materials, but also the cost of

In February 1901 the GWR *Magazine* reported on: 'the latest example of the genius of the Company's Superintendent [Churchward] "The Great Bear" which is of the "Pacific" type and is the first of its kind in Great Britain.' It caused great excitement, but Ernest Fischer has a special reason to remember the Great Bear because of the worry it caused his family:

> My grandfather was a boilermaker. He worked on the splashers that went on the Great Bear. Apparently there was a fault in the drawing and when they made these splashers they wouldn't fit. He was so worried about it he couldn't eat his dinner at dinner time, just sat and worried about it, but it turned out it wasn't him, it was a fault in the drawing. So he was let off.

No wonder poor Mr Fischer was worried. He was probably thinking of Rules and Regulations No.21 which states: 'Any workman making an article of wrong dimension ... may be called upon to make good such work and be liable to a fine of 2s 6d or to instant dismissal.' Such a worry would put anyone off their dinner.

time not spent on 'proper' railway work. When the workman left the Company, all tools issued by the Company had to be inspected and returned, as was the key to his drawer or tool box, and the workman was not paid until this was satisfactorily completed! In 1874 Rule 23 specified: 'Every mechanic is expected to provide at his own costs all the special tools necessary for his work, such as rules, callipers, compasses, squares etc.' This rule still stood in 1904 but with the extra imposition that the workman must also 'insure his own tools' as the Company would not be responsible for 'any destroyed or injured by fire'. Whilst the Company expected the workman to provide these special tools they were also very clear that using 'the Company's time, tools and materials for private use', i.e. to make them, was strictly forbidden and would incur a fine (2s 6d in 1904), suspension (i.e. loss of pay) or instant dismissal. Despite these threats many apprentices, with the help of a mentor, liked to make pieces for their own use which would take them through their working lives. One such apprentice who took his chance in the 1940s was Ken Gibbs, who remembers that though this was still completely unofficial, a 'blind-eye' was turned on account that such things would help the lad in his future work. With the 'nod' and help of his fitter journeyman, Ken made his own callipers and scribing block, which he still proudly has today. This 'using the Company's materials' was a situation that neither the GWR nor whatever arm of British Rail that subsequently ran the Works, ever won. Making use of what was available in the factory had taken root in the 'foundling' days of the Works, when there were no shops offering such materials and little money spare to buy what there was. These were 'creative' men used to creating extraordinary things from metal and wood and therefore it was, seemingly, a natural progression for them to 'create' for their own needs. It was a tradition that was to become part and parcel of being an 'Insider'. 'Foreigners' as they were called, i.e. anything made in the Works that wasn't 'official' were part and parcel of the 'underground' workplace culture that continued right up until the Works closed. Many, if not all, ex-Works' families, from the lowly to the highest, have treasured 'foreigners' either purely practical – leather wallets, iron pokers, wooden doors, to crafted furniture or even conservatories; or sentimental, such as a brass 'key-of-the-door' bearing personal initials presented on one's twenty-first birthday; or even attractively ornamental pieces, such as brass or copper vases, all of which have then been handed down through the generations. Roy Taylor remembers:

> Everyone used to get foreigners made up. I remember this chappie, in No.8 office, the Managers' Office, Mr N., the clerk, he'd called me a 'silly old fool' for not taking the fitter's job my dad had arranged. 'You're a silly b***,' he said. Sometime later he wanted a foreigner done, when I was in the Welding School. I said 'I'm not sure whether to do it, I remember when you called me a silly old b***! He said 'I don't remember that.' Anyway, I did it.

John Moxam recalls being advised by 'a sympathetic mate' to look in a bin of scrap taps outside O Shop when he needed a tapered (No.1) 7/8th Whitworth tap, for one particular 'foreigner' he was making, while Jack Fleetwood, who used to work in the Foundry, remembers he was very popular just before Trip, as people wanted carriage keys made so that they would not have to hang around and wait for the officials to open them. Having the key meant they had a head start over other trippers in claiming a particular carriage, and was an added boon if it was raining, which it often was! Even the female employees would make their own 'foreigners'. Clive Wilson's Aunty Joan worked in the 'Sewing Shop'. 'She would make us anything, curtains, cushions, tea towels, anything my mum needed.' Brian Maddicks couldn't believe it when he started as labourer on the 'heavy gang' in 1961. From Bristol, Brian was an 'incomer' and completely new to the Works and its 'make-it-yourself' culture. He was, he says, 'bowled over by the people in there. It was a fantastic place to work, like a family concern. You could get anything done or made in there. I never knew anything like it.' A way of 'controlling materials', i.e. stopping things leaving the Works that shouldn't, i.e. pilfering, was by controlling entry to and from the Works' site and where men were on the site, both during working time and during meal breaks and these issues were often referred to in Notices and circulars.

Another major reason for these controls was to do with safety. This was a never-ending problem for GWR and later BR. The Works was an extremely dangerous environment and there were frequent accidents from people taking short-cuts and being in the wrong place at the wrong time. A circular dated 15 December 1894 identifies one-such incident:

Fateful Accident to Blacksmith William Clarke at Swindon 30th October 1894
On the morning of the 30 Oct. last Mr Clarke was crossing the line on his way to the Engine
Shed to work, he was knocked down by an engine and killed.
Clarke was 75½ years of age and had been in the service of the Company 40 and 7/12
years, his rate of wages was 6/- a day. He has left a widow in very poor circumstances, she is
practically dependant upon a married daughter for support.

As such this was a 'problem' that was liable to a heavy penalty. Fred Jell went into the Works
shortly after Nationalisation. Even then going in the wrong entrance was a sackable offence:

When I started all I can remember is the six chimneys of the Rolling Mills. You could see them
from all around. I went in the wrong entrance. I went in the tunnel entrance and I crossed over
the main lines. So I headed off to the chimneys. The man said, 'You could have been sacked
on the spot, crossing them lines. That's a sackable offence, that is.' I should of gone in the other
entrance. There was another entrance down Sheffield Street, under the Carriage side.

There are several rules that relate to safety and working practices such as No.31 (1904):

The moving parts of any Engine, Crane, Lathe or other machine must not be oiled or cleaned
while in motion. The parts of the lathe or machine must not be changed while in motion. No
workman must attempt to put on a strap or interfere with the main shafting in anyway while
the engine is in motion.

Pretty commonsense one would think, but the tone of the penalty highlights the fact that
this must have happened, with dire consequences to machine and or man, on a number of
occasions. It states: 'Any workman who violates any provision of this rule will be considered
guilty of serious and wilful misconduct and to have rendered himself liable to instant dismissal.'
Rule No.33 states: 'It is most important that workmen employed on lathes and other machines
should wear close fitting jackets.'

Non-compliance with 'close fitting clothing' was still causing problems in 1930 despite
threats of dismissal. Circular No.3369 is quite mild in its admonishment considering the
circumstances:

Factory Acts Regulations for the guidance of Workmen – Clothing
Several cases have recently occurred where accidents have been due to clothing being caught
in machinery. This principally applies to jackets with loose sleeves being worn and I shall be
glad if you will take immediate steps to ensure that the following regulations are complied
with: Clothing – No-one be allowed to work any kind of machine in loosely fitting clothes.

The GWR Rule Book persisted up until the GWR's demise in 1947. After Nationalisation
there were a number of significant differences in the new Rule Book (apart from it now
being the 'Resolution of the Railway Executive' (1950) and later the 'Resolution of British
Railways Board' (1972) and addressed to 'employees' rather than 'workmen'), significant ones
being that there was not now a specific 'Works' book and the imposition of fines had been

dropped. Now the sub-parts of each rule were far more numerous than before, having to be applied so generally to the whole of British Railways. Other disciplinary practices such as the newly worded 'dismiss without notice' are continued, while 'suspension' is applied to more situations. Some rules such as not bringing intoxicating liquor to work, absence from duty without permission and returning company property when leaving, span the time. The general consensus of the workmen I have spoken with is that post-1960, whilst the rules existed, there was a lot more leeway in them. One could receive a number of 'verbal warnings' but the sting had gone out of them. There were more mechanisms for 'appeal', and the unions were more powerful in fighting the worker's cause and so, significantly, there were very few dismissals.

Tin Gods in Bowler Hats

The foremen were the most feared men in the Works. As one man put it: 'In the beginning there was God, and he was called 'the foreman'. From the beginning and even for a good number of years after Nationalisation, for the men in the workshops it was 'the foreman' whose word or nod mattered. In modern-day terms they were 'the main man'. This is not an overstatement of the power that these men had as those who worked with them well know. Right from the beginning, when the Works' Manager or Superintendent wanted something seen to, he would inform the foremen of his or the Company's wishes and expect the foremen to see them done. The foremen were 'the enforcers'; they enforced the 'Rules and Regulations'. Circulars addressed to foremen always spoke of 'your shop', 'men under your control', 'your men', leaving little doubt as to who ran the show. The extent of their power is highlighted in the wording of the 1874 Rules:

> Infraction of the following Rules will be punished *at the discretion of the foreman* [my italics], either by discharge, suspension or fine, the extent of the penalty being determined according to the nature of the offence, but no fine will in any case exceed 5/-.

With the foreman lay the power to inflict loss of earnings and punitive fines as well as the supreme power of 'hire and fire'. In early times the foremen were a law unto themselves, and Management as well as the men had reason to fear their actions, as a somewhat curt and exasperated circular sent to 'all foremen' in 1859 shows. It states:

> I find some of the foremen have been deciding for men & promising them a certain wage without my knowledge, it is impossible for me in all cases to bind myself to these promises. I shall be glad if in future you will make no stipulation whatever on wages without first seeing me.

So annoyed is its author that he has left it rudely unsigned, but undoubtedly it would have been from the Managers' office. Over twenty years later in 1882 Management seeks to stop the practice of 'men who are seeking employment' being brought to the shop to 'see the foremen' by the employees during meal hours, whilst Circular No.456 of January 1899 shows the move towards a formal 'take over' of recruitment procedures by the Managers' Office:

New Men Starting Work

Please note that commencing on Monday next 23rd inst., our present arrangements for starting New Men will be altered as follows:-

When you require a man to start in your Shop, instead of sending him direct to the Sick Fund Office to pass the Doctor as hitherto, please instruct him to come to the Manager's - Accounts Office at 9.0am on either Monday, Tuesday, Wednesday or Thursday, in order that his antecedents may be ascertained – before any further steps are taken towards engaging him. If then approved he will be at once sent to pass the Doctor, or if there is any delay occasioned by the particular circumstances of any man's case you will be duly informed.

Decades later Ernest Radway writes of his foreman when he was an office boy in 19C Shop in the 1920s: 'George Mann had the name of being very strict with the men under his direction. He was indeed an imposing figure with the right to hire and fire.' Even when they had lost this power, they could, remembers John Walter, 'make or break you in terms of your career prospects, particularly as apprentices.' 'Tin Gods' was a much-used title for this special grade of men and, undoubtedly, they could make your life easier or make your life hell as John Attwell remembers: 'The foremen and chargemen were the people with influence – and we were at the mercy of which one we got.' It was the foreman's prerogative to decide who was put in which gang, who was in charge of the gang, and which gang were given the 'best' jobs at the best prices. J. Silto writes in *The Railway Town* about the Works from 1901 to 1918 that: 'it is sometimes suggested by disgruntled workers that favouritism played a big part in the selection of foremen and that attending the right church, having a relative in a good position and being a Freemason or "Yes-man" were some of the reasons for promotion.' He also suggests that some men curried favour with their foremen, or head foremen, who could give small pay rises, with 'discreetly offered small gifts such as freshly killed rabbit or newly picked mushrooms … or even to dig the foreman's garden or paint his fence.'

We have a good idea who the first foremen in the factory were thanks to what is known as the 'Fawcett List' which was written out retrospectively by John Fawcett (a contractor) in 1865.[3] An earlier 'Notice' dated 21 July 1856 from Minard Rea giving authorisation for contributions to a disaster fund for 'the widows and orphans who lost their relations in the awful accident at the Cy– Clothing Ltd.', makes interesting reading as it lists the 'Foremen and Contractors' to whom the men's donations should be handed in. The listed men are particularly interesting in that there are certain 'discrepancies' against the Fawcett List, but we know for sure, however, that those as identified by Rea as men to whom his instructions should go, were definitely in the Works at that time.

Foreman and Contractors

On 1856 Notice	As identified on Fawcett List
Mr Walter Mather	Second Foreman of Erecting Shop
Mr William Nicholson	First Foreman in Fitting & Turning Shop
Mr Thomas Stewart	Second Foreman in 'Smiths' Dept
Mr William Falconer	First Foreman of Wheel Turning Dept

Mr Richard Pattison	Third Foreman of Erecting Shop
Mr James Haydon	Third Foreman in Fitting & Turning Shop
Mr Thomas Rawlinson	First Foreman in Paint Shop
Mr Samuel Gray	First Foreman in Patternmakers Dept
Mr Robert Laxon	First Foreman in Coppersmith Dept
Mr Thomas Jones	First Foreman of Masons Dept
Mr John Fawcett	First Contractor having taken all Wheel/Tyre repairs under Mr Sturrock
Mr William Hogarth	Second Contractor for New Engine Wheels
Mr William Laverick	First Contractor for Steam Hammer Work
Mr Joseph Thorpe	Succeeded Mr W. Hamilton [*Hamilton not on Rea's Notice*]
Mr Smith &}	[*Smith not on Fawcett List*]
Mr Bremner}	Contractor for building Iron Trucks when Brack /Tilley left [*Brack & Tilley not on Rea's Notice*]
Mr Creasy}	Made all Wooden Frames, doors etc. for the above Iron Trucks
Mr George Hawkins}	

VIPs: homberg, bowlers and trilbies show the status of these men. Ted Plaister, head foreman of A Shop, sits proudly centre stage. From left to right, back: Foreman Wally Dew, Mr Raven AM Shop, -?-, Foreman Millard. Front: Foreman Boilershop, -?-, Ted Plaister, -?-, Chargeman P1 Shop.

With the tradition of sons following father into the Works, a small number of families could boast a foreman down through the generations, often stepping into their forebears' shoes. Circular No.28 of January 1891 informs that: 'Mr F. Laxon has been appointed to succeed his late father as foreman in the K Shop'. A smaller number still, such as the Plaister family, could boast several foremen at the same time! John Walter and Roger Hayes were both foremen in the latter days of the Works; both had 'foreman' in their blood. John's father, Jack, was a boiler maker, who became foreman and later head foreman, of the Boiler Shop Group, *c.*1948. Both Roger's grandfathers were foremen before him. Grandfather Hayes was foreman of the Locomotive trial gang which tested locomotives following general repairs in the workshop and grandfather Godsell was foreman in C & W workshops. Both men went on to become head foremen at the same time and appear in the official photograph of 'Officers and Foreman' 1931 taken outside the Main Offices. These official photographs were taken every ten years and make fascinating perusal, capturing as they do some of the great names in the 'management' history of the Works. In 1941 John Walter's father appears under the heading of 'Officers & Foreman Swindon Works' and three decades later in 1971 John can be found under the heading 'British Rail Engineering Ltd. – Swindon Works' Foremen's Association and Senior Management.' Roger says of his grandfathers: 'in their days foremen were known as 'the unapproachables'. They would never speak to subordinates and you only spoke to them if you were spoken to. When the foreman left his office to walk down the workshop, the word would pass down between the men in a matter of seconds, so by time he arrived in your area, everyone had their heads down and were working hard.' If you were a lowly journeyman who wanted to 'get your head down' it was easy to spot a foreman as they were instantly recognisable by the way they dressed, especially their distinctive 'trademark' – the bowler hat! Hugh Freebury described the foremen in the Platelayer's Shop in the 1930s:

> The Platelayer's Shop – one end was the D Shop, the carpenter's shop and the other end, the PL shop. It had four foremen … more than the largest workshop of all, the AE Shop. The Head Foreman Street was a true Victorian character, short, stocky and proud of a white handlebar moustache most conspicuous against his florid complexion. Second Foreman Jefferson, a man of few words, Foreman Woolton and 'Home' Foreman Stanley Bruton. All these important individuals were immaculately turned out: Street and Burton in their navy blue, Jefferson in grey while Woolton inevitably favoured thick tweeds. And, of course, each sported that hallmark of foremen everywhere, the traditional bowler hat.

The earliest, although 'unofficial' photograph to be found in the GWR's *Magazine*, of the 'Locomotive' foremen on an outing in 1895, shows almost all but a couple of the thirty-six sporting a bowler, the others have top hats! Brian 'Bob' Gale remembers even when he started in the Works in 1952 one of the first things that struck his attention was the headwear of the men, even then he says: 'the head foremen usually wore bowlers, the under foremen trilbys and most of the shop floor men flat caps, although the bowler hats were beginning to die out, in fact the last foreman I think I saw wearing [one] was Mr Mittens in the AW Shop where I worked later on.' Both Roger Hayes' grandfathers wore the trademark – in their day a *black* suit and bowler, but by Roger's time this 'dressing up' had gone. 'I never wore a bowler or a suit like my grandfathers. I wore something much less formal.'

The role of the foreman, particularly the head foreman, as well as being one of stern authority, carried a great deal of responsibility, how much depended on the size of the shop or number of shops or department under his command. A.E. 'Dusty' Durrant wrote:

> The chief foreman, Mr Millard, presided over a gathering of under-foremen each with his group of charge-hands under whom came various tradesmen, apprentices and labourers. I do not know how many men were employed in A shop, doubtless well over a thousand, yet railway practice called the man in overall charge a mere foreman! In most places one-tenth of a size, outside the railway, he would be called at least works manager, or even works director.

To be a foreman one had to have 'something about you', as 'foreman' was on the top rungs of the ladder on the shop floor. For most the career pathway from apprentice to qualified journeyman (or craftsman or tradesman – all meant the same) to leading-hand in a gang, to chargeman, to inspector then senior inspector, temporary foreman to foreman, and on to the dizzy heights of head foreman, who could be in charge of a large shop or several shops, then, in the later years, even superintendent (this was not a superintendent over the Works as in the days of Gooch, Armstrong, and Dean, but still a very senior 'shop-floor' management role) took many years, but just a few made it more quickly. Stan Read was one. He started his apprenticeship in November 1939 as a 'fitter-turner-erector and millwright'. He was one of the last to do so as 'millwright' work, which required working with timber, was later re-designated and absorbed into carpentry. Being in a 'protected' trade, Stan could not join up, but his skills were put to use 'out-station' at just nineteen and by twenty-two he was in charge of an outstation 'gang of four', himself, a fitter and two fitter's mates. Marriage and a youngster on the way brought Stan back 'Inside' around 1949 where he took up a post as fitter in G Shop. Just over a year later he became chargeman on the maintenance gang and a mere sixteen months later on 17 June 1953 he was 'made-up' to foreman, earning the princely sum of £570 a year. He then worked his way up to become an 'outstation' district foreman in 1955. Interestingly in this post Stan exercised the foreman's old right of hiring labour, even going to the Labour Exchange to discuss what men he required. In May 1960 Stan moved onto the Test House, working on the development of lifting equipment for the new diesel engines. Later, when they changed production schedules, he was transferred to the AE Shop in charge of a bay. He then had a short spell down at Eastleigh before returning to Swindon and finding a temporary home as instructor at the Works' Training School but was soon asked to work on the development of the new facility for removal of contaminated material, i.e. asbestos. As Stan says, 'this was the time everyone was becoming scared of it'. The job involved decommissioning the old Asbestos House, with all its inherent dangers, and building the new house with the latest decontamination equipment available. Stan's last move was back to his 'roots' in the Millwright Shop, G Shop, where he stayed until the end of the Works. Stan's 'something about him' was knowing when to listen and organisation, right down to the last little detail. In his capacity as Secretary of the Foremen's Association for a goodly number of years, Stan used these skills to organise numerous well run outings and functions.

To go beyond foreman took you into the 'special' grade. An inspector was a grade 2, a foreman a grade 1 and a head foreman started at 'Special A' grade up through to 'Special C' grade. Becoming a superintendent took you into the 'MS 1' grade, i.e. Management and Supervisory grades. Ken Farncombe was one of these 'super' men and amongst the first to be so. Ken had followed his grandfather, Frederick, an electrician, or in the early days a 'wireman', who had come to Swindon from Brighton to work on electrifying Queen Victoria's royal coach, and then his father, Frederick junior, a fitter, into the Works in 1939, apprenticed as a fitter/turner on the C & W side. Later in 1947 Ken left the Works for a short time but returned in 1948. Viewed as a 'new starter' again, he was moved here, there, everywhere, wherever filler-ins were needed. Some ten years and several shops and jobs later, he was 'tried-out' as a temporary foreman over a two-month 'probationary' period (which was standard practice) and then made up to permanent foreman in 15 Shop which had at this time (1958) six gangs of around fifteen to twenty men in each gang, one of which was the bogie-gang whose chargeman was Ken's own father, Fred. This could have been a difficult situation for father and son, especially as Fred was known to have 'his own way of doing things'. 'He was a perfectionist and would personally inspect every bogie in his charge and if he didn't like the workmanship, he wouldn't let it go, no matter what the foreman thought,' Ken remembers. 'Up 'til then he was always the one that gave me the orders and said what went, but now, in the factory, that was my job, but I was prepared and knew how to avoid getting on the wrong side of him.' It was an exciting time to be a foreman in 15 Shop in charge of diesel multiple units. This was a milestone in the Works' history along the path from steam to diesel. Ken oversaw the build of the first four 'Schlieron' (later known simply as the B4s) bogies which were to eventually become the standard bogie for use on British Rail. In the days before the Works' 'Planning Office' all 'planning' and scheduling for 'marking off' work took place through negotiations between the foremen, the unions and chargemen in the various shops, of which Ken was now part. In 1962 Ken was promoted to 'Special A' grade foreman for 'Maintenance' on the C & W side, then to 'Special B' grade in 'Saleable Machinery' in 1964, transferred to 'Works Study' for a period in 1965, then moved back to 15 Shop. After a spell in 11 Shop on the Loco side Ken was promoted to 'Special C' grade in No.3 Fitting and Machining Shop. Shortly after this, after yet another Works' restructuring, Ken was again 'made up' in March 1970 to become one of the first newly introduced superintendents. Superintendents 'oversaw' a number of different shops that undertook similar-natured activities. The shops under Ken's jurisdiction were the Machine & Fitting Shop, the Tool Room, the Pattern Shop and the Brass & Aluminium Foundry. Made up to a MS2 grade in 1973, the Blacksmith Shop, the White Metal and the Heat Treatment shops were added to his list. His final promotion to Superintendent MS3 Manufacturing, extending his responsibilities even further, was in April 1983 a few short years before the final closure. There were five other Superintendent positions – Machinery & Plant Maintenance; Wagons; DMU & Coaches; Engines & Gearboxes; Locomotives.

Foremen came up through the ranks so they knew the work and they knew the nature of the men on the shop floor and they knew the tricks that could be pulled. 'Jack' Fleetwood remarks:

> Your knowledge of the jobs involved in the shop was a great asset as a foreman, as you would always get chaps trying to pull a fast one, 'the machine will not work' or 'this furnace is very slow melting', but if you could show them that the machine was working perfectly, they would not try that one to pull the wool over your eyes again.

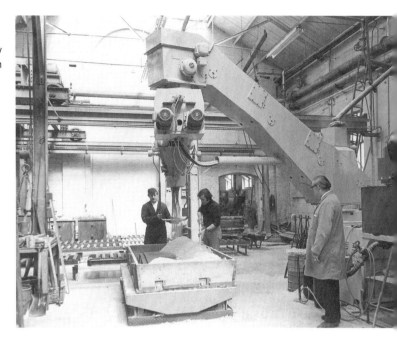

Jack Fleetwood, on right, seen here overseeing the new air-set-mixer, making doors for new carriage stock, was the foreman of the brass, iron and 'white metal' foundries. Jack states: 'because conditions in the Brass Foundry were not ideal, control of these men had to be handled with skill' (c.1970).

Whilst outside the Works, within their families these men could have been as lovable as the next man, 'Inside', especially pre-1950s, they maintained a stern face and discipline and in GWR days were often the managers' secret police. Circulars marked 'Private' were nearly always to do with clandestine behaviour to be carried out by the foremen as with a Circular of 1871 instructing them to surreptitiously check to see that all people who said they were there, were actually there, and again in Circular 3483 of November 1932:

Private – Factory Discipline

When selecting men for discharge we are handicapped by the fact that there is no record in writing of those cases where men have not conducted themselves satisfactorily in the shop or have been guilty of other offences which would single them out for discharge when it is necessary to reduce hands.

In a number of cases where questions have been raised it appears that the foreman has, on more than one occasion, reprimanded the man verbally, but you will realise that in the absence of any definite particulars in our records it is difficult to substantiate such cases when discussing them with the Trade Union representatives.

In future therefore, I shall be glad if you will send me in a report on any man under your supervision where conduct in any particular or whose ability to carry out his work is not satisfactory.

Signed R.G. Hannington

Alfred Williams wrote of the foreman's 'Black List' and woe betide any who got on it – you might as well pack up and leave. Cyril Godwin recalls an incident when he was an apprentice in the 1930s where his foreman enforced the rules in an emphatic way, without even having to say a word:

One thing that stands out in my mind is about Steve 'Stivvy' (not called this to his face) Hale, the foreman in K Shop. He used to come in at 9 o'clock and not 8 like us. We weren't allowed to knock off at ten for a cuppa or anything then, so we would have a look-out see if anybody was about, before brewing up a cup of tea. One day this journeyman was brewing up on the bottom fire. He said 'Stivvy isn't in yet' but who should turn up? Well the journeyman dashed off outside but Stivvy spotted that brew-up and stood there so-called warming his hands in front of that fire. He waited for the can to boil dry, then he waited for the can to melt right down to a molten mound, then he just walked up the shop to his office, half way up the shop on the side wall. He didn't say anything.

Mr Hale had other ways of keeping his men and apprentices on their toes which Cyril clearly remembers, being the target of one of them:

Stivvy used to have the boys who didn't go to night school up to his office, give them a good talking to. I was working with Joe Parsons, the journeyman, and Joe said, 'you won't be going up there.' I said, 'No fear, I go to night school regular' but then a lad came down said, 'Mr Hale wants to see you in the Office.' I thought 'what?' The Shop head clerk used to sit alongside Stivvy and at that time the head clerk was Charlie Godwin, my great-uncle. There were three steps up to the office and I stood on top step waiting to be called in – he always kept you waiting. Charlie looked behind Stivvy at me and gave me a look, to let me know it was alright. Stivvy said, 'Ahh, that's got them all talking, I know's full well you go regularly.' Well that was 4.30 p.m. and we finished work at 5.30. I got home before my father, who worked in A shop, and when he came in he said, 'I hear you've been up before Stivvy. What you been up to – playing truant?' I said, 'No I haven't, you can ask Uncle Charlie what he heard' and I told him, 'I think he did it to keep everybody on their toes' but it shows how quick that grapevine worked. Stivvy was alright if you toed the line, but if you didn't obey all the rules, he would come down on you like a ton of bricks.

John Moxham, an 'incomer' Premium apprentice from London in the early 1940s, remembers very clearly the impact of one particular foreman, and recounts in his memoir *Apprenticeships in Life*: 'In the T Shop there was a martinet of a foreman, and, without exception, all were afraid of him. He would exercise his authority by riding his bike on factory premises right into the shop and dismount at the foot of the office steps.' Obviously as with any group of people, there were some foremen who had a more 'human face' and one we get to know through the pages of the then *Temperance Union and Great Western Magazine* in the late 1880s/1890s is Mr W. Harvie, the head foreman over the women employed in the C & W Polishing and Trimming Shops. There are a number of reports about the women's 'annual tea' at which Mr Harvie puts in a jovial presence. After the tea there is entertainment put on by the women themselves and in which Mr Harvie joins with at least a couple 'of humorous songs' which are said to 'greatly add to the success of the evening'.

Mr Harvie is variously described over the years as 'the popular foreman', or 'the respected foreman', he is also a very gentlemanly foreman as he remembers every year to compliment the ladies on their endeavours, surpassing himself in 1892 when he commented that, 'he was surprised and pleased that the ladies were so clever as to get up such an excellent dramatic performance.' His female workers also had their own 'forewoman', at that time probably a Mrs Turner. In the 1940s Mrs Kath Grayhurst, who worked as a French polisher, remembers a Miss Woodruff. Even with the women, the position of 'forewoman' set them apart, as Kath recalls: 'We hardly ever spoke to the forewoman, and certainly not in a familiar way. She was a lot older than the rest of us but it just wasn't done. She ruled with an iron rod. Very strict. A big distance between her and the rest of us.'[4] In October 1945 the GWR *Magazine* carried a small item regarding the retirement of Miss K. Fagan who had worked for twenty-five years as the forewoman of the 'lining-sewing staff and axlebox pad makers'. It told how: 'Representatives of shop Nos 9, 9a, 10, 10a and 19a, recently paid tribute to the splendid way in which she had fostered team spirit.' Miss Fagan was presented with 'a wallet of treasury notes' by Mr W.E. Duck, foreman, on behalf of the shops and office staffs.

One of the early foremen who was obviously held in high esteem was Edwin Thomas Brittain. Edwin was born in St Pancras, London, in 1829. He learnt his trade as an 'engineer' with the London & Brighton Railway, then worked for sometime at Wolverton with the London & North Western Railway before arriving in Swindon in 1853, aged twenty-four, with wife Louisa and young son Thomas Edwin. They lived first in Taunton Street and then, from 1865, in King Street. Louisa and Edwin had twelve children altogether, six boys and six girls. Three children died in infancy. Four of their sons followed Edwin into the Works – Thomas Edwin 'an engineer' (sub-contracted by the GWR for work on railways in South Africa) who died in 1890 from the dreaded consumption; Charles Wilbur, a pattern maker who also died wretchedly of, it is believed, cholera, at just eighteen years and five months in 1874; then Walter and Henry, another pattern maker, who is reported in the *Magazine* as having given a talk on 'Pattern Making' to the Engineering Society in 1908. Edwin did well, as 'Mr Brittain' appears on list of a foremen on an official circular dated 1859. In 1865 he did even better as he became assistant foreman in Joseph Armstrong's newly constructed and much admired R Shop, the 'Machine' Shop, first under Mr James Haydon, then under Mr E.J. Davies, being finally 'appointed to the chief foremanship' himself in 1875. Edwin stayed in this post until his death aged sixty-five from 'apoplexy' (stroke), as certified by Dr G.M. Swinhoe on 27 June 1895. His obituary in the *Swindon Advertiser* informs that: 'for many years nearly all the fitter-turner-erector apprentices received their early training under his management … those trained under him are to be found in most countries in the world where engineers are found.' The reason we know Edwin was held in such regard is because of his 'Memoriam' headstone above his grave in Radnor Street Cemetery. A tall, impressive pink stone obelisk, similar to Cleopatra's Needle, and similar to that erected commemorating Joseph Armstrong, it would have cost a tidy sum. The paper tells how nearly 400 people followed Edwin's coffin from the church to the graveside and the route was lined with respectful spectators. The article remarks that his 'position in the Works was unique [being] the oldest foreman in the Works' and that 'he was a very old employee'. Although sixty-five seems a young age to us today when thousands live to over 100, we must remember that in those days people generally died a lot younger, especially in the railway village. Although extremely short in stature, Edwin had obviously made a big impact. Family member Mrs Wakeley says: 'he was known to be a very, *very* hard man, but also very fair.'

Edwin Brittain (seated at front), foreman in R Shop from 1865 and chief foreman from 1875 till his death in 1895, was held in particular high regard. His specially commissioned obelisk in Radnor Street Cemetery reads:

In Memoriam
Edwin Thomas Brittain
30 years foreman 'R' Shop
Loco Dept., G.W.R.
Erected by Present and
Past employees and
Personal Friends as a
Token of Affectionate
Esteem.

Ernest Fischer was lucky to find his foreman's 'soft-side' otherwise he could have lost an afternoon's pay! He remembers: 'If you were late in the afternoon, you weren't allowed to start that shift that afternoon. One day my cat followed me back to work after dinner, so I had to take it back. Then I had to see the foreman, but luckily he said it was alright, because of the cat.'

Obviously, along with all the responsibility, being a foreman came with some 'perks' like bringing your bike into your office and not leaving it in the bike shed. One also didn't have to arrive in the 'Works Mad Rush' but could sign in at the entrance several minutes later and, at the other end of the day, could also leave the shop just before the official finish time and be ahead of the rush! In August 1907, however, F.G. Wright writes a 'Private' circular to all foremen and assistant foremen, curtailing this 'privilege' owing to the fact that as soon as the foremen are gone, 'the men leave off work before the hooter blows … as there are no foremen to check them.' The privilege must have been reinstated because Jack Hayward remembers foremen still leaving 'early' when he went 'Inside' in the 1950s. Perhaps an even better privilege in the days of primitive facilities, the foremen had the key to a special locked water closet and in later years special foremen's amenities rooms were introduced in some of the shops. Whilst all GWR workers had entitlement to 'privilege' tickets, i.e. travelling at discounted prices, foremen of the highest grades could travel first class, along with their wives and young children! Foremen could also give play to their own particular thinking or even superstitions. Albert Dawes remembers that one foreman in the Iron Foundry would never allow anything to be cast on Friday 13th. 'It became accepted practice. It just wasn't done and everybody knew this!'

Another significant 'perk' was that the foremen had their own association. A report in the *Magazine* in 1895 tells of probably the first 'organised outing' by 'the Loco Dept Foremen' on Saturday 24 August. It informs: 'about 35 foremen' presided over by 'senior-foreman' Mr L. Dyer visited Gloucester and Symonds Yat. A good day was had by all and they 'declared it would not be fifty years before they had another' and indeed it was not, as the outings became regular annual events and continued even after the Works closed. It was the beginnings of what was to become an association for all the Works' foremen. Operating under the ethos of 'to work with the officials in a spirit of amity' it was initially an official instrument to facilitate policy and practice between management and men. The foreman's role in this was, to quote from a report of its Annual Dinner in 1925, to: 'apply in a practical form, the ideas and instructions of the management' and, after 1965, they were also involved in the overall planning and implementation of training matters. The Association also looked out for its retired members, seeking to alleviate any financial difficulties of those in dire distress. It also had a

The Swindon Loco Works' Foremen's first outing to Symonds Yat on Saturday 24 August 1895. From left to right, back row: D. Clark, J. Townsend, C. Tincknell, J. Thomas, A. Nash, R. Pattison, G. Dingley, W.S. Sheppard, D. White, C. Tigh, W. Morgan, R. Harris, W. Hunt, S. Thrasher (hon. sec.), F. Hopkins. Middle row: T. Veness, W. Chivers, H. Hayward, G. Willis, T. Watson, L. Dyer, J. Burrows, R. Baker, F. Apted, E. Noad, J. Hunt. Front row: F. Laxon, J. Faulkner, T. Patterson, J. Smith, A. Mizen (set back), G. Webb (Managers Office), G. Townsend, B. Hale, (set back) H. Barrett, G. Seath, T. Hardiman.

very active social side with an 'Entertainments Committee' which arranged the annual dinner and excursions; latterly, when the unions took over more of the 'liaison and mediating' role in the early 1950s, this became the Associations' primary function. John Walter, the presiding president, gave a 'vote of thanks' at the Association's final gathering in January 1991.

A foreman's retirement was a notable event and often written up in the *Magazine* or local paper. One such event in February 1899 is recorded under the heading 'RETIREMENT OF A G.W.R. FOREMAN – Interesting Presentation' regarding Mr William Morgan, who had been at the Works for forty-three years, of which he had been foreman for twenty-nine years and nine months, firstly in V Boilersmiths' Shop and latterly in Q Smiths' Shop. It tells that Mr Morgan had made good use of his experience in the Works and in 1874 invented and then further improved upon it in 1884, a 'Hot-air Tuyere for smiths' forges which was a great boon to all who used it … saving much fuel and water.' The 'interesting presentation' was a purse of gold and an 'address contained in an album'. These 'addresses' were calligraphic works of art and highly thought of at the time. Mr Morgan acknowledged the gift and replied that he 'had always tried to do his best towards those under him and at the same time his duty to his employers'.

The power of the foremen and their relationship with the men changed considerably after the Second World War, not least because the returning men had seen a different world. The profound experiences that people had been through, whether at home or away fighting, had changed them and their willingness to 'put up with everything' so they began to challenge

It seems somewhat ridiculous that the GWR were worried about men smoking in the midst of all the 'fires' in the Works but up until the Second World War it was a punishable offence. By the time of this photograph taken in the Foundry in 1981 (showing a cupola being filled with molten metal from a hydraulically tipped furnace), men working with a cigarette clamped between their lips was commonplace.

many of the old conventions and expectations. Percy Warwick recalls how such changes, often small in nature, began to make a significant difference:

> During World War Two work was contracted to outside firms who came into the Works, like in 15 Shop, there were people in there doing gun turrets. They didn't have to put up with what we did. So things changed. Before the war we had no official breaks, you had to catch your 'lunch' when you could, but during the war they started an official break in the morning and a ten minute break in the afternoon. When I started you couldn't smoke, but when outside people started coming in, they were under different rules to us and they could. Then one Monday we were told we could carry on smoking. Lo and behold there was the foreman walking around smoking. You couldn't smoke anywhere, not where there were fire hazards, like the Trimming Shop, the Paint Shop and the Carpenter Shop.

The unions had become more powerful during the war and had won many concessions from the Government for the benefit of the railwaymen and women. Nationalisation also brought big changes. This was now a company owned by the people (i.e. the taxpayer) run for the benefit of the people, who were also the people who worked for it. Alongside this was the steady influx of 'incomers' to the Works; the Polish and the Italian POWs during the war; the ex-servicemen after the war; the 'London over-flow' in the 1960s, who did not come with the baggage of generations of family allegiance to the Company and the 'inbuilt' acceptance of handed-down traditional

Robert 'Bob' Townsend went into T Shop (Machine Shop) in 1962 when he qualified as a fte – fitter, turner, erector. He remembers:

> because of the transition over to diesel at that period not many people finishing their apprenticeship wanted to go on turning, especially because the new diesel work gangs were getting more 'balance.' I applied to go to the BD Shop but got dragged up by the foreman in the Brass Shop. He didn't want me to go. He wanted me to take over the Mud Plug Automatic machine … ['mud' plugs are actually made of brass and used in steam boilers] so I really got my wrist slapped.

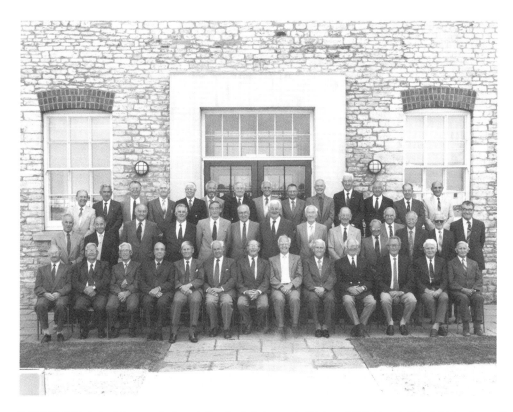

British Rail (Swindon) Foremen's Association final photograph, 25 June 1993. From left to right, back row: ? Waldron, S. White, G. Turner, C. Rayer, W. Turner, D. Barnes, J. Findley, G. Culling, E. Nash, D. Raven, B. Carter, G. Nash, F. Pearl, J. Tyler. Middle row: K. Jones, A. Fall, P. Chambers, J. Hayward, J. Perry, R. Taylor, A. Rudden, L. Edwards, F. Monk, K. Farncome, J. Fleetwood, R. Jones, F. Vellender, H. Hacker. Front row: C. Godwin, R. Taylor, H. Cox, R. Tuckwell, W. Yeo, A. Elliot, S. Read, J. Walter (president), D. Mayall, W. Read, K. Witts, W. Cook, R. Pritchard.

practices. Although for those who started their apprenticeship, or who came to the Works after these events, the foreman was still an awesome presence, his power had subtly diminished and the nature of the foreman-workman relationship had shifted. A good example of this step-change difference was, as Percy Warwick recalls, 'when you started calling the foreman by his first name. When I started if you saw a bowler hat you were gone, now it was "hello Charlie"!!!' Cyril Godwin became a foreman a few years into this increasingly relaxed time:

In 1959 I put in for foreman's job as he was retiring and got that job. When I was an apprentice the foreman, Walt Mittens, of the Wheel shop, always wore a bowler. The Managers use to come round wearing a bowler. We used to say "if you came out from underneath an engine and there's a bowler hat around, watch out". Things were a bit more flexible when I was made up. We didn't wear the hats. There were tea breaks by then. We just had to make sure they didn't stay at it too long. There was still the respect though.

These more 'relaxed' times also came with more union intervention (Ken Gibbs remembers in the 1960s that, on informing the foreman in R Shop that a Work Study was to be undertaken to examine the reasons for the bottleneck on cardon-shaft repairs, he discovered that the foreman couldn't just give the go-ahead, they had to first check it with the shop-steward); the foremen had to find other ways to operate and use more than just 'fear' to control the men. 'Negotiation' became a necessary skill and requirement. Stan Read maintains that one of the essential skills of a foreman was to know when and how to listen as: 'sometimes when there are complaints, they are valid. You need to be able to pick out the wheat from the chaff.' John Walter says of being a foreman in the 1970s: 'then it was acceptable and expected to be "one of the boys" maybe, sometimes, a little too much.' Even as late as the 1970s, however, the foremen in 15 Shop were known as a formidable group of men who looked out for each other, so much so, it is whispered, that they were generally called 'the Mafia'. Later still Roger Hayes remembers how in his foreman period 'we were more approachable. You had to be fair and know your job to get respect. By the time I finished at the Works in 1986 it had become a completely different affair.'

Undoubtedly, from its earliest times, foremen played a significant role within the Works and stamped a GWR imprint on the work culture of its shop floor. Their role in the history of the Works deserves fuller attention.

'The check' and 'the checky'

Time was a precious commodity for railway companies. It was one that was at the forefront of their thinking for, as the old saying goes, 'time is money', particularly in terms of traffic and production and money was something that the GWR were always short of. The GWR, so often a leader in railway matters, led the way in 'railway time' for it was the GWR who, on 3 November 1840, introduced 'London Time' to their train timetables and, eventually by 1852 throughout the whole of their system, whether in Leamington Spa (approximately seven minutes behind London) or Penzance (almost fifteen minutes behind). This was, of course, very helpful for the GWR but rather confusing for those residing up and down the system who had then to function on both 'local time' and what came to be known as 'Station Time' the time shown on the big station clock! In September 1847 'London Time' so called because it was delivered from the Royal Observatory in Greenwich, London, was adopted by the Railway Clearing House and over the following years was taken up by most of the railway companies. It was still not, however, 'official' or 'legal' time but was observed by the companies by mutual agreement. Greenwich Mean Time or GMT (i.e. London Time) was not universally popular and some towns adapted by having the expediency of not one but two minute hands on their notable clocks. Oxford's illustrious Christchurch's Tom Tower clock and the clock over the old Corn Exchange in Bristol were two such, the latter where the black minute hand showed Greenwich Mean Time and the red minute hand showed Bristol time! GMT was not legally adopted as 'standard' time on mainland Britain until August 1880 which gave us British Standard Time (BST) after which 'local time' no longer officially existed. The GWR established a practice whereby the 'time signal' was received from Greenwich at 10 a.m. and instantly transmitted throughout its system. All lines of communication were kept clear purely for this purpose for two whole minutes before the signal was due.

To say the GWR were great sticklers about time and timekeeping is something of an understatement; to say they were fanatical, would be nearer the mark. Everyone and every thing had to be on time. Deacons Jewellers in Old Town Swindon, although not given the main contract for the Works, were sub-contractors for timing equipment which varied from signal box timers to guards' pocket watches and were the main contractor for the Midland & South West Junction lines that ran from Birmingham New Street to Andover. They still have in their Wood Street showroom the Deacons 'Regulator Clock' which has a mercury pendulum that expands and contracts depending on any change in pressure and temperature and thus compensates for any time loss or gain, ensuring infinitesimal accuracy, against which all their timepieces for the GWR were specifically tested. Down the decades the GWR Notices and circulars return again and again to the matter of 'time' and 'timekeeping', particularly in respect of what they held to be 'poor' timekeeping or misuse of time records. In the early days of the Works the men had several 'start' and 'end' times during the day, and, it would appear, that sometimes their 'starts' were not precise enough. Works' Manager William Gooch is very precise about the time and the minutes when he wrote to the foremen in August 1857:

> In addition to the present system of ringing the bell for summoning the workmen, it will in future be rung a second time beginning 3 minutes before each hour, that is 5.57 a.m., 8.57 a.m. and 1.57 p.m., and continue ringing for a further 2 minutes. The door will be closed punctually at the hour and the special attention of all workmen is called to Rules 6 & 7.

Before 25 December 1871 when the '9 Hour Day' system was adopted, with fifty-four hours constituting a full week's work (incidentally this was celebrated by the Works' men with a parade through the town), the men worked through until Saturday afternoon. In 1875, Rule 6 shows the start and finish times of the then working day:

Monday to Friday	6.00 a.m. to 8.15 a.m.
	9.00 a.m. to 1.00 p.m.
	2.00 p.m. to 5.30 p.m.
Saturday	6.00 a.m. to 8.15 a.m.
	9.00 a.m. to 12 noon

To help 'control time', the Company initially employed men who were called 'TimeKeepers' to collect the workmen's time-tickets and record their timekeeping. This was the first organised system of 'checking-in' and 'checking-out' (later known as 'clocking-on' and 'clocking-off'). Later the GWR introduced a system of 'metal tickets'. Rule 8 (1875) explains:

> Each workman is furnished with a brass ticket having his number stamped on it which he must himself deposit in the box appointed for the purpose every time he returns to his work. If he neglects to do this he will be paid half-time only for that particular portion of the day. If any man deposits the ticket of another workman he will be discharged immediately and the man who requests or allows another workman to deposit his ticket, will be dealt with in the same way.

The warning bell would ring (later it was the hooter that would blow) and then the men who failed to check-in exactly on time, each time, would lose a quarter of an hour's pay. In July 1869 Mr Carlton wrote to his three 'Time Keepers' Messrs N--pes, Young & Baker instructing them: 'In future please stop the ticket of any person losing the 3rd quarter in one week so that they cannot again commence work until they have seen me.' The 1916 Rule Book shows that workmen who had lost their 'ticket' had to report it to the ticket man and pay a sum of 6*d* for a new one. Over time these 'brass time tickets' numbers had to be used along with the man's name on any 'vouchers' to do with time-records, wages, transfers or fines as a means of 'checking' the information. Later the metal tickets became known simply as 'checks'. The 'checks' were hung and deposited on a board known as 'the check-board'. The GWR's *Magazine* described it as: 'like a show-case with rows of small hooks and with a front glass panel that slides upwards to open.' It was manned by 'the checky' – i.e. the 'Timekeeper' or ticket-man had become 'the checky' but still with much the same role. In the early decades the GWR had used their Timekeepers to 'police' the workmen, even

Each shop/shed had its own check-board at its entrance. The check-board was manned by a 'checky.' What is a 'checky?' Andy Binks who was 'Inside' in the 1970s explains:

At the start of the day you had to 'check-in' using a brass check with your shop number engraved on it, transferring the check from the outside to the inside of the board. All these boards were manned by what was known as 'checkies'. Some of these men were particularly strict and even if they saw you coming and the clock had just ticked over to 7.31 am, [7.30 start time] which meant you were late, they would slam down the glass panel on the 'out' board and quickly hang a 'quarter check' on your peg on the 'in' board. This meant you were docked a quarter of an hour's wages at the end of the week. If you were more than a quarter late he would hand a 'see foreman before starting' check. The foreman could then have said 'you will not start work today' and you'd be sent home, which meant no wages for the day. (David Hyde Collection)

You could distinguish which 'side' of the Works the men worked on from the shape of their check, rounded bottoms for Loco side and heart bottomed for the C & W. Besides the men's own individual checks, special quarter- (green) and half- (red) hour time checks were introduced to be hung on some poor unfortunate's hook indicating his lateness, which meant he was docked a corresponding sum of money. Ken Gibbs has collected and preserved this fine array of the various types of checks.

using surreptitious methods to 'catch out' the men who may have been manipulating their time records as a circular of January 1871 to all foremen, marked '(Private)', shows: 'In order to check the attendance of your men I wish you to have a list of their names and go round your shop occasionally and mark the names of those who are absent, then ascertain from the Timekeeper whether their tickets have been put in or not. Report to me any cases of irregularity you may discover.' Another 'policing' role that the Timekeepers played around this period, this time in conjunction with the Works' Policeman was to prevent any man with a 'lighted pipe' entering the Works, as smoking was then strictly prohibited, even during meal breaks. In later years, the 'checky' played a similar 'policing' role, as Percy Warwick remembers: 'When I went in there first in 1939, under a certain age the starting time was later than the usual and I can always remember the checky coming up to me the night before my birthday saying, "You'll be 15 tomorrow so tomorrow you start at 8 o'clock" and I had to start like the rest of the men.' As Percy found out, 'the checky' knew everyone and everything about everyone! It was this that made him a useful member of the shop and the reason behind workshop slogan 'See the checky, he'll see you right'. Percy also remembers that the only 'quarter' he ever lost was because of his daughter! 'It was when my youngest daughter was born. When I phoned up the hospital in the morning they had advanced it and it was all over, so by time I'd been round to see my mum and her mum to tell them, I was a bit late and I lost a quarter.' The 'Timekeeper' or the 'checky' were not the most popular of men as Clive Wilson's Uncle Sid would acknowledge: 'He tried to be a bit sympathetic and turn the occasional blind eye,' remembers Clive. 'Blokes would say, "which shift you on Sid?" He was from Rodbourne, and he hated it having to go and work at the main entrance,' remembers Clive. 'He called it a "foreign" part of town.'

The GWR were not only determined the men should get *in* on time, they were also equally determined they should not get out *before* time. Even when the foremen appear to be being helpful in allowing certain less-able workers to leave a few minutes early to beat the rush, Circular 281 dated 30 June 1896 shows that the Management wanted to ensure no person was let off without their authorised permission:

> **Men leaving the shops before time.**
> I notice there are several employees (either old hands or cripples) who leave their shops before the hooter blows at 1 o'clock and 5.30 respectively. I wish to obtain a list of all such cases and will be glad if you will send me a memo giving me the names of any persons in your shops who have the privilege and the reason why it has been allowed to them so that I may consider each case on its merits and prepare an authorised list.

For the rest of the men and boys even leaving the shops then waiting at the entrance gate for the hooter to blow was definitely not acceptable, as Mr Carlton emphatically informed his foremen in September 1871. This issue of the men leaving before the *exact* time continued to annoy the Management and it appears again and again in the Works' Circulars.

The use of 'the check' continued until the introduction of 'Time Clocks' and 'clock cards' by BREL on Thursday 22 April 1976. Each worker received a letter of notification and instruction from the Works' Manager, Harry Roberts, instructing them how to use the new system and which number clock was designated for their use. Amazingly the letter also informed them that they had a 'lateness allowance' of four minutes at the start of each shift *without incurring any penalty* – a massive change from previously when a minute late meant a quarter lost! Penalties no longer came in quarter- or half-hour slots, but were broken down more minutely:

> If you book in at 7.35 a.m. you will lose five minutes pay. From 7.36 to 7.40 a.m. you will loose ten minutes, from 7.41 to 7.45, fifteen minutes pay and so on. After 8.00 a.m. take card from 'Out' and see Shop Foreman to obtain permission to book 'On' duty. The Foreman will record the time on your card … [and] inform the Time Recorder Attendant. At lunch-time Staff will book 'On' up to 1.34 p.m., without penalty, after 1.34 p.m. you should clock on and then obtain permission from the Shop Foreman to commence work.

The letter included instructions regarding the handing in of their brass 'time check' when booking out on the Wednesday, and information that 'these will be hung on the check boards on Thursday and if you wish you can claim this as a souvenir.' Many men did so. Although not particularly fond of the 'checky' the men came to have a special fondness for their 'check' and many ex-railwaymen can still rattle off their number! The copper 'pay checks' were continued a little longer. These had been first introduced on Friday 4 February 1898 under 'New Pay Arrangements' whereby the men no longer signed the 'Pay Bill' at the Pay Table in acknowledgement of their wages, but instead had to give up this special metal check. One of the 'happier' jobs of 'the checky' was to collect the copper pay-checks from the pay office on the Thursday afternoon and exchange them on the check-board for the ordinary time-check every Friday morning in order that the 'giving-up' could happen. On Thursday 6 May, the clock card took over from the 'special metal check' and was then used as receipt for wages. On pay day two cards were in the rack, the current one in use for clocking on, and the previous one for which payment was being made. This was the one that had to be handed in, in exchange for the wage packet.[5]

Clocks and 'the Clockie'

Whilst the GWR expected very close attention to timekeeping by the clock from their men it would appear that before 1896 there was no coherent policy of having an allocated Company clock in each workspace as Circular No.292 dated 14 August 1896 signed by George Webb for Churchward and addressed to all foremen signifies:

> Please let me have by Monday morning at 9 o'clock at the latest on the enclosed form, a list of the clocks in use in your shops or department. Please say in each case by whom the repairs to the clocks are executed. Please say whether the clocks were supplied by the Company or purchased by the men. This must apply to all clocks, whether in Office, Shops or Sheds.

This was a situation they obviously intended to address. Over the years there came to be a great many Company clocks all over the Works as those who worked there remember, mostly situated within the foreman's or the shop clerk's office. There were so many clocks that one skilled man, known to all as 'the clockie', was employed to wind all the clocks once a week, which took him every day, Monday to Friday. He had a winding rota of which clocks had to be wound each day and as he went around he had a special watch, his mobile master clock, to re set and adjust the individual clocks to. On two days of the year, when the clocks went forward and when they went back, he was at his busiest! According to John Plaister, a local expert on the clocks inside the Works, the clocks varied from spring-driven English dial clocks, all timepieces in drop or round cases, to a few weight-driven clocks. All, except the weight-driven clocks, had English fusee movements. There was only one official clock in the Works which had a passing strike on it, which just sounded one note each hour, and this clock was reputed to have been in William Dean's office, when he was Works Manager. This clock, which is now in STEAM Museum, was made by Dell of Bristol and could have joined the clocks in the GWR when the Company took over the Bristol & Exeter Railway. 'The clockie' also executed any necessary repairs and carried out annual maintenance checks on the clocks, on a small workbench within the O Shop (the Tool Room) in the Loco Works.

He also twice weekly wound the only large public clock associated with the Works which was situated on the tower of the Mechanics Institute. This clock was made by Vulliamy of London. It was able to strike the hours but this was stopped owing to complaints from the people who lived in the Company houses. People often have difficulty recalling the clockie's name as they never called him anything else, but Head Foreman Frank Millard remembers that 'the clockie' during the 1950s–1970s period was 'Jim' Richards, and that he did a nice line in unofficial 'trading' repairing and cleaning personal watches or clocks as well as selling watches, which were kept discreetly hidden in a hanging coat. There was a 'clockie' employed 'Inside' right up until the Works closed and indeed his knowledge assisted in the final collecting in of all the clocks.

Whilst their early clocks were all mechanical the GWR, always keen to engage with new technology, introduced in the early nineteenth century a new 'electrical system' to operate the clocks. John Plaister tells how:

> Around 1912 the GWR installed two master and slave clock systems with a master clock in both the Locomotive Works and the Carriage and Wagon Works that each had slave dials in some of their main workshops. The master clock system was self-generating. It made its own electrical pulses to move the slave dials and this was done through the mechanical clock movement rotating a magneto, generating a small current every minute. The magneto was similar to those on the very early motor-cars. These clocks caused an uproar with the workmen as these clocks were very prominent and the men thought they were going to be 'watched'. When the Carriage Works was closed, the wiring system for its master clock was broken up and the clock was moved to the entrance in the main Managers' Offices as a centre piece. The Locomotive Works' master system continued until the late 1950s when it was replaced by Reading Clock Shop with modern gent slave dials controlled from the master clock in the Works Telephone Exchange. This master clock is now in STEAM Museum.

After the installation of this new clock system the GWR sought to rationalise its clock situation in the Works. In May 1913 Collet wrote to the foremen: 'Please let me have the following particulars of any clocks or timepieces (not including the Magneta dials) in your shop. Position, description, no. of dials, measurement of dials, makers name & number, condition. I shall also be glad to know if any of the clocks can be dispensed with.' Eventually each clock had its own GWR number engraved on a fixed ivorine plaque.

There were hundreds of timepieces in the Works and when the Works finally closed, all of these were gathered together for sale. The man charged with this duty was the then Technical Services Manager, John Walter, who recalls:

> Some of the clocks were rare collectors' items which concerned me so I had a discussion with the Works' Manager Harold Taylor and suggested that I remove all clocks to a secure area over one weekend without prior notification and he agreed. I had a meeting to organise the collection with the Chief Watchman, Dennis Cooper, and the fitter (the clockie) who maintained all the Works clocks and knew where each one was situated. I then arranged for three workshop staff and a transport driver to work with me out of hours but not told why as security was also high on my list. I prepared a note authorised by the Works' Manager for

the removal of the clock that I placed in the position of each removed clock and then one evening we collected every clock and secured them in a prepared area of the Wages Office. After collating details of the clocks they were offered for sale through the BREL Supplies Organisation at Derby.

According to John Plaister the Management at Derby had planned to sell the clocks in one tender but after relentless badgering by railway clock enthusiasts Derby agreed the clocks could be sold separately, so these clocks have ended up scattered throughout the country. Richard Deacon recalls how he visited the Works with his father Michael, to find that twenty of the collected clocks had 'Deacons' on the dial face. They had wanted to bid for these in one lot, but, sadly for Deacons and Swindon, they were not allowed to. These Deacons clocks were, John explains, mostly sited within the GWR Medical Fund buildings, i.e. the hospital and the swimming and Turkish baths. There is, he adds, one other rather touching story relating to a particular clock in the Works. Following the First World War the men of what was known as 21 Shop, C & W side, purchased a clock to hang in their shop, in memory of their fallen colleagues. This was mounted on its own Memorial Board stating: 'gifted by the men of this shop in memory of their colleagues lost in the Great War.' This clock was not owned by the GWR and as such did not have a GWR ivorine plate and number on it. The clock in 21 Shop came across to the Loco Works and into the L2 Shop when the Carriage Works were closed but its final whereabouts is not now known.

The winding of GWR's clocks was not a job for the faint hearted. For their station clocks the GWR insisted that it required 'a competent person to perform the duty, and see that it is properly done' and Circular No.808 of June 1883 dictated by J. Grierson, General Manager, gave eight very specific instructions as to how this was to be carried out. Instruction number two informed: 'Greenwich time will be transmitted daily from Paddington to all Stations at which a telegraph instrument is fixed.' For the GWR 'Greenwich Time' was not only observed on their railway lines but also in their railway offices and workshops as instructions dated 7 August 1928 show:

> To ensure regularity during short time working when the hooter is not being blown, please arrange … for the ticket station man to obtain the correct time from the Shop Office before the termination of each spell of duty and see that the check boxes are not opened until the closing time is reached.
>
> Greenwich time can always be obtained by your Office Staff upon application to the Telephone Exchange.

Time meant money and for the GWR, who lurched from one critical financial time to another, money was not something to be squandered. An article entitled 'Mechanical Time Recorders' in its *Magazine* (1922) states: 'Perhaps at no period in the history of the world has *Time* meant as much as it does today when the nations are striving to balance the economics of the world by production.' Production and pay went together. Pay structures for the workshop men were always complicated even in modern-day times. There were always a great number of elements to be factored into the equation, and it was crucial, therefore, to the man as well as the Company – especially in early times when pay day only came each fortnight – that strict time records were kept in order that he would get paid fairly and the Company would not pay out too much. Rule 9 (1875) tells that 'a small book is supplied to each workman' for this purpose. In 1902 Rochester Time Recorders were introduced causing some sense of grievance amongst the workmen but the Trades Council after obtaining reports from the various unions considered it inopportune to move in the matter. Even when pay was paid at a weekly rate it was still necessary to know when the weekly 'hour rate' had been fulfilled before any overtime was calculated and Rule 7 (1916) states: 'each workman must enter in the book or timesheet provided for the purpose, the name and description of the work on which he has been employed during the previous day, and if on more than one job, the time on each. Any workmen neglecting to enter the time correctly or to deposit the book or sheet at the proper time or place, will be liable to a fine of 6d.' Such work records were always important but more so when the men were on 'short-time' and every penny counted.

Whilst 'time and tide' may wait for no man the GWR had endeavoured to control 'time' as much as they possibly could. After Nationalisation the workers still had to keep to time, but it was not so stringently controlled to put men in fear of their jobs. Whilst it was still not acceptable to amass too many ¼s, no one felt that it was going to hurt them too much, apart from in their pocket. In respect of time spent on any particular job, it is said that the 'time and motion' studies popular in the 1970s played more into the hands of the men and unions, than to the benefit of BR and so, in this respect, the balance of 'controlling' time had shifted.

'The Hooter'

One of the more memorable methods that the Company used to 'control' the men and their timekeeping grew to have its own story which has become a legend in its own right and earned a special place in the history of the Works. 28 October 1867 marked a new and mighty sound amongst the cacophony of noises that already resonated around the factories. Originally the railway workers who lived close by in the village were summoned to work, and finished work, by means of a large bell, fixed to the roof of C Shed. The enforcement of the 'rule of the bell' was strict and severe as notices issued by Minard Rea show:

Swindon Works 22 April 1853
Copy to all the Foremen & Contractors
Last evening I observed men leaving off work before the 6 o'clock Bell rang.
I beg therefore, to call your particular attention to this great irregularity which must immediately be stopped.

General Notices
Men leaving off work before the Bell rings will be discharged from this employ.

By 1867 the Works and New Swindon had grown and many of the workers now lived further afield, even in outlying villages, too far away to hear the bell. Another means of letting them know the work hour was nearing had to be found; remember this was an age when very few had watches or even clocks. A 'Steam Whistle' or 'Steam Trumpet' as it has variously been described, mounted on the roof of the 1864 Fitting and Machine Shop (R Shop) over its steam engine power house, came into use in October of that year, and its sound 'neither louder nor more piercing than other such steam whistles' according to the GWR, could be heard many miles away, but particularly, all the way to Lydiard Tregoze.

Each morning the steam whistle (which eventually became known to all as 'the hooter') would summon the men to work and then mark the course of their day. Its schedule was:

At 5.20 a.m. for a period of 10 minutes
At 5.30 a.m. for a period of 3 minutes
At 6.00 a.m. for a period of 1 minute
At 8.15 a.m. for a period of 30 seconds
At 8.50 a.m. for a period of 30 seconds
At 9.00 a.m. for a period of 30 seconds
At 1.00 p.m. for a period of 30 seconds
At 1.50 p.m. for a period of 30 seconds
At 2.00 p.m. for a period of 30 seconds
At 6.00 p.m. for a period of 30 seconds

Looking back and especially in respect of the problems it created, it makes one wonder why it was necessary for the hooter to 'blow' for so long, especially given the fact that it was undoubtedly loud enough to wake the sleeping, no matter how deep a sleeper! Jack Hayward, a regular contributor to *North Star*, the magazine of the 'Friends of STEAM', believes that it was probably just continuing an established practice. Its predecessor, the bell, not nearly as loud, would have been rung for such a long period in order to maximise its 'alarm-call' for the workers. The sound of all this hooting, however, was not to the liking of all and in 1868 Henry St John, 5th Viscount Bolingbroke had had enough and complained bitterly to Joseph Armstrong, Superintendent of the Works. Anxious to placate Bolingbroke, Armstrong engaged in 'an immense amount of correspondence' with him, eventually inviting him to tour the Works, hoping to convince him of the need for the 'steam trumpet', but to no avail. Bolingbroke appealed to the GWR Directors who agreed to muffle the hooter with a surrounding screen. One feels sorry for the GWR as, in soothing one set of ruffled feathers, they ruffled many others. Now it was the turn of the men and other locals who had come to look to the whistle for their timekeeping to complain that the dampened sound was not up to the job, so the screen was scrapped.

Amidst all this controversy Samuel Carlton, Locomotive Works' Manager, reasserts the authority of the hooter schedule as well as the consequences for not obeying it in March 1869:

On and after Wed 31st inst., I have arranged for the Factory Whistle to be blown at 6.0 am, 9.0 a.m., and at 2.0 p.m. so that no excuse can be made for men not commencing work at the right time. Please inform your men of this and any persons not commencing work at the proper time after this arrangement will be severely dealt with.
Signed S Carlton.

The words 'Lord Bolingbroke' and 'Swindon Works Hooter' have become notoriously linked together. Try as he might the mighty Lord did not win 'the battle of the hooter' and, happily, the will of the people prevailed.

LORD BOLINGBROKE AND THE SWINDON HOOTER

*"Will any doctor or physician come forward and say
That the health of this gentleman is going to decay
Through the sound of a trumpet vibrating the air?
No, not one on his account will come, I declare."*

In 1870 the 'clergy, landlords and tenant farmers' of fourteen parishes or districts, all residing within six miles of Swindon, including Wootton Bassett and Lydiard Tregoze, Bolingbroke's districts, sent in petitions requesting the continued blowing of the factory whistle 'as usual' as it was 'a great boon to Master and men', so the GWR continued to use 'the ordinary steam whistle' but with greatly reduced timings – the 5.20 and 5.50 a.m. calls lasted not ten, but just one minute and the others a mere three seconds. Despite the fact that he is said to have spent a mere two months a year at his country estate, Lord Bolingbroke was determined to have his way and silence what he called the 'loud piercing, roaring and distracted noise'. He again appealed to the GWR Board who then ordered a different hooter to be installed 'the tone of which was not so loud'. A Company Notice dated 7 June 1872 informs: 'Commencing on Monday next the Factory Whistle will be taken down and a Locomotive Guards Whistle fixed in its place.' Still not satisfied Bolingbroke formally applied to the Local Government Board in February 1873. In response to Bolingbroke's petition Swindon New Town Local Board had to put forward to the Right Honourable James Stansfield MP and the Local Government Board the reasons for their granting the sanction to use the whistle, requesting that this should not be revoked. Recalling the now infamous incident in his book *Swindon: Reminiscences, Notes and Relics of Ye Old Wiltshire Towne*, William Morris suggests that Bolingbroke: 'set up some sentimental personal grievance of his own against the convenience of some five or six thousand working men: when he objected to the use of a steam whistle for calling the thousands of workmen to their labours on the grounds that its noise might possibly frighten and disturb a few of his pheasants sitting on their eggs a few miles off.' Bolingbroke's application for the whistle to be stopped set off a real hullabaloo that sounded as loud and as far as the whistle itself! At a packed and rather heated meeting at the Town Hall in Old Town in June 1873, the Local Government Board Inspector, Mr Longe, listened to the one objection and the one witness, i.e. Dr Cooper, who gave medical evidence that Bolingbroke was 'prejudicially affected' as the lack of sleep was detrimental to his weak heart, and he was requesting that 'the hooter must not blow again'. The locals were outraged. How could one man's wishes outweigh 'the express wishes of town and neighbourhood'. Many wrote to the paper, one summoning up the feelings of many of the workmen:

> I have a wife and four children, wages 16s per week, and being a sound sleeper I am satisfied I should lose many mornings quarters if the whistle was discontinued. I do assure that I can scarcely make both ends meet, and to lose a quarter or two would be a great loss to me and my family.

Twelve months later in February 1874, having heard nothing from 'the Right Honourable Board' a meeting held at the Mechanics received massive support from New *and* Old Town. *The Swindon Advertiser* reported that one attendee wittily commented: 'The workmen might as well say when they had their trip to London that Big Ben should be stopped!' The chairman of the meeting, Mr W.R. Wearing, reported that they had been to see the Hon. F.W. Cadogan (MP for Cricklade which then included Swindon), who had informed them that all they had to do was switch one hooter for another. Joseph Armstrong then announced that 'the Company was constructing a new hooter, not a steam whistle but an atmospheric one.' On 7 July 1874 the Local Government Board eventually delivered their verdict to 'revoke the sanction to use such Steam Whistle or Steam Trumpet as from the First day of August 1874,' executed under the Nuisances Removal Acts. As William Morris wrote in his editorial on 13 July 1874, 'the victory rests at present with the noble Lord.' Happily the new atmospheric hooter (like Brunel's atmospheric railway) used air, not steam, so the ruling did not stop the blowing. Curiously the new hooter was said to be even louder. It is claimed that on a clear day it could even be heard in Devizes! Ironically, Lord Bolingbroke died peacefully in his country house at Lydiard at the grand age of eighty, so his 'weak heart' hadn't been too troubled!

Some time later, the hooter (which was actually two hooters – one for near sound, the other for distance) was re-sited on the Central Power Station, at the north-east corner of the boiler shop, which became known locally as the 'Hooter House'. It also reverted again to steam. An official 1892 hooter drawing identifies it as such and it is a steam hooter that became the iconic landmark within living memory. Around 1960, the water capacity in the Works was reduced and the water tank, against which the hooter was fixed, was dismantled. The hooters were then fixed to the side of the building with an additional supporting rail. During this their height was lowered and the manner in which they 'blasted' changed. Cyril Godwin, then foreman of K Shop, remembers that at this time K Shop supplied new 2¼in pipes and that the controls changed from a ball valve to a tap valve, all of which had the effect of a slower start at a reduced pitch leading to a gradual build up to a full head of steam. The hooter now slowly rumbled into effect rather than opening its lungs and blasting.

Down the years 'the hooter' established itself as part of the railway identity of Swindon. As Jack Hayward eloquently writes: 'At a time when an unpretentious Swindon throbbed to the rhythm of its huge industrial hub, the Works' hooter imparted its own tempo to the lives of countless

Generations of Swindonians grew up knowing that a seventeen-second blast of the hooter meant it was 6.45 a.m. and time to be up, and if they were not inside their shops when they heard the beginning of the last twelve-second blast it was 7.30 a.m. and they were late.

SWINDON WORKS HOOTER				
	MONDAY to THURSDAY		FRIDAY	
	TIME	DURATION	TIME	DURATION
M O R N I N G	6·45	17 SECS	6·45	17 SECS
	7·20	12 SECS	7·20	12 SECS
	7·25	7 SECS	7·25	7 SECS
	7·30	12 SECS	7·30	12 SECS
	12·30	12 SECS	1·30	12 SECS
A F T E R N O O N	1:05	12 SECS		
	1·10	7 SECS		
	1·15	12 SECS		
	4·30	12 SECS		

Swindon families over many generations, who had little option but to heed its beckoning calls bringing them to and sending them from work each day.' In 1875 Hubert Deacon advertised his new line in watches as 'the watch that keeps hooter time' and in 1895 the 'Loco Dept., Foremen's Outing' still kept to 'hooter time' when they regrouped for lunch at Symonds Yat. John Walter holds, like many others: 'I suppose being born in the GWR maternity home in Milton Road in 1929 and living my early days in Rodbourne within the sound of the hooter made me a true railway child.' Even when clocks and watches were more common in use, Swindon people and railway families still regulated their lives to the sound of the hooter. Timed against an ordinary clock checked daily with the Works Telephone Exchange, the hooter sounded to a carefully orchestrated timetable. As the working time changed, the pattern of 'blowing' was changed too.

Writing of the early 1900s, Joseph Silto tells how at the end of the day's work as 'the last reverberating sound [of the hooter] died away, a new sound could be heard – the thudding of feet as hundreds of running men raced through the tunnel … all intent on making their way home. It was the 'Works Mad Rush' and local people knew to stay out-of-the-way until it was over.' Writing of the 1930s and '40s Eric Mountford recalled how: 'The sound of the hooter was a daily feature of the town; life was controlled by it … meals got out of the oven and dished up in readiness for the menfolk when it blew.'

Despite people's memory of the hooter sounding unfailing everyday, Circular No3249 dated 7 August 1928 shows there were times when it didn't. It informs that special action must be taken to determine 'the correct time of termination of each spell of duty [while] during short- time working the hooter is not being blown.' To do this shop office staff had to obtain 'Greenwich Time from the Telephone Exchange'. The lack of the hooter must have reinforced the impact of the lack of paid work on people's daily lives emphasising their dependence on the Works. The hooter was to play a different 'tune' and significant role in Swindon people's lives during two particularly notable periods: the two world wars. Permission was given that: 'the Hooter may be used at any hour for military signals and such signals will be given by a number of short blasts' and so ten blasts announced the beginning of the First World War to Swindon in

Mr H. 'Joe' Owen operating the controls for the 12.30 dinner break, November 1962. 'Joe' and Arthur Franklin, a fellow 'hooter-man', confessed it was strange being both the most popular men – at going home time – and the least popular men – at getting-in time – in the factory. Here we can see all the paraphernalia involved in blowing the hooter – the clock, the timetable, the pressure gauges, the pipes and the turning wheel. (David Hyde Collection)

1914 and thereafter six short blasts announced 'an emergency'. During the Second World War it was again brought into 'military' action. An ARP Notice issued by the CME's Department on 30 June 1939 announced: 'Air raid rehearsals will take place tomorrow night, Saturday July 1st between 10 p.m. and Midnight when the Works' hooter will be blown at the commencement and finish of the practice.' According to Mr Harold Millard, one of the long-serving 'hooter-men', it was sounded nearly a thousand times between 1940 and 1944 to warn the town. Even after Nationalisation the hooter continued its daily calls. In 1960 the *Swindon Railway News* staff magazine wrote an affectionate article under the heading 'The Voice of the Works' declaring:

> There is really only one hooter. Other local industries have whistles, sirens ... some even boast hooters of their own; but their puny pipings bear no comparison with the full-throated bellow of the Works hooter. It is the voice of management issuing clear and definite instructions in plain and simple language. Twice daily it says 'Come', twice daily it says 'Go', and we come and we go.

The article tells how Arthur Franklin, who did daytime duty on the hooter, had notched up some 14,000 hoots to his credit, which if blown in one long blast would be equal to forty-eight hours! It informs that as with every 'legend' there are the 'small' stories of those who 'did it their way' and 'the hooter' story is no different. There is the one about the lad who nipped in and blew the hooter at 11 a.m. causing confusion and consternation to all, and the embarrassing one about 'someone' who caught his sleeve in the wheel (before the time of the safety locking device) and let off the steam four minutes early (perhaps this was the reason for the safety locking device!). It ends stating that: 'Swindon would not be the same without the old hooter's clarion call.' It was a prophetic statement.

The last sounding of the hooter heralded the final closing of the Works. John Walter was the man in charge of this iconic operation. He tells the story of the dramatic final minutes:

As Technical Services Manager it was my responsibility to ensure that the shutdown of services was carried out correctly and safely. Finally the day came for the Last Hooter Blow. I was determined that it should be a little special. I visited my Boiler House 'B' chargeman and explained that I would like a full head of steam from the one boiler on line that day and what I proposed and which I also discussed with the Power House attendant. I knew that the

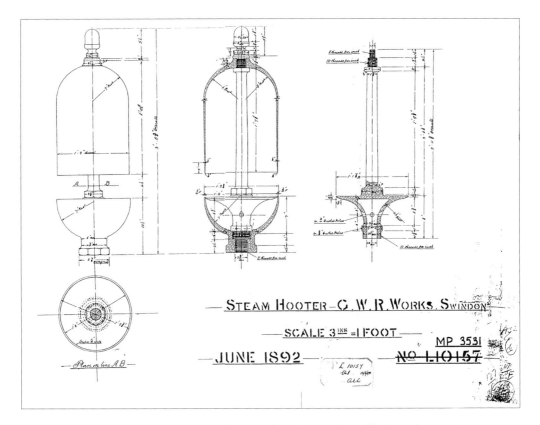

This magnificent technical drawing shows the exact dimensions and specifications of a new *steam* hooter, which it remained until the end. (David Hyde Collection)

Jack Hayward recalls: 'the hooter was a magnificent sight in full blast. Reminiscent of a mushroom-shaped cloud, its plume of steam rose majestically white against a clear blue sky, but if you stood in its shadow you could find yourself doused in a misty spray.' Few people got as close-up to the working hooter as did maintenance fitter Andy Binks, who took this photograph during a lunchtime blast whilst working on the roof area, c.1980. 'It is hard to believe that those two things made so much noise,' says Andy. 'It was like a hollow booming sound but strangely I wasn't deafened.' In this picture we can see the frame that supported the hooter pipes after the water tank was taken away (c.1960).

attendant should have the 'honour' of opening the operating valve for the last time and only shutting it finally when all the steam from the boiler had been exhausted, I wanted the sound of the historic Swindon Works Hooter to slowly die away to nothing and then forever keep silent. And that is how it happened. All that remained was a faint trace of steam drifting away in the wind.

From a personal aspect I was surprised at the length of the 'blow' so with the attendant's agreement I operated the valve to give three short separate blasts in memory to my late wife who had worked as supervisor in the Works Telephone Exchange, and then handed the valve back to the attendant for the final closing.

When 'the hooter' sounded for its last time at 4.30 p.m. on 26 March 1986 it was a momentously sad moment for many Swindonians as years of history were carried away as steam and sound on the wind. Swindon folk had come to have a special relationship with this 'cry of steam' that issued its commands. It had become, as expressed in a poem written in to the Swindon Advertiser in 1873, 'our friend – the factory hooter'. Many again wrote to the Papers to mourn its passing and pay a final tribute. Again a number felt drawn to commemorate it in verse. Mr Warrick Forrester of South Marston wrote:[6]

The Hooter

They say the hooter's silent
And there's no more work 'Inside'
With all the ghosts departing
The railway works has died
No hammer blow or scrape of file
Or rivets resonant ring
No oily toil work skilful hand
To service 'Tank or King'.

The say the hooter's silent
No cabs or wheels or frames
No 'molten' on the 'balance'
Or cast and gleaming names
No showing of impatience
The blast of steam and smoke
Just a whistle down the distance
Beloved of Swindon folk.

The say the hooter's silent
As the Adver' has remarked
The sidings rails are rusting
The workshop still and dark
Like a heart that's finished beating
A way of life now gone
No matter what the future brings
The hooter – echoes on.

In Fear and Trepidation!

Controlling the workers to a certain degree, even if just for administrative or safety reasons, was obviously necessary especially when the numbers were so great – 14,000+ at their peak, but the ways of control appear at times somewhat excessive, especially in the GWR era in the early 1900s.

When looking at Alfred Williams' choice of words in relation to the workmen being 'terrorised' and 'subjugated' they may, at first, appear a little extreme, but from the earliest times and certainly during his time, the workmen were undoubtedly 'threatened' at every turn – threatened with fines, threatened with suspension and loss of pay, threatened with dismissal and threatened with the loss of their home, so it is easy to understand why he, and they, would have felt this way. These railway 'servants' were kept very much aware of the hierarchical power structures and their role of 'servitude'. Even after the 1950s the Rule Book still carried similar 'threats'; time-management was still practised and exercised through the checky, the Time Recorder, the hooter and then through time-and-motion studies; the workmen were still subject to instant dismissal, albeit it then happened very rarely; and the foremen were still employed to 'control' the shops. What had changed significantly though, was the power base had shifted and the attitude of the men towards all this 'control' had altered – the terror had been abated.

Endnotes

1.   Chandler, 2005.
2.   All information and quotes relating to Parker and Freebury taken from Freebury 1985.
3.   Peck p.198. (See Bibliography)
4.   Matheson, *The Fair Sex: Women and The Great Western Railway*, 2007.
5.   All information taken from interviews, Company circulars, GWR Magazines, Ken Gibbs' article.
6.   Information on the hooter taken from booklet issued by Borough of Thamesdown; the *Swindon Advertiser*, David Hyde's artefacts; Company Circulars and official documents in private collection.

CHAPTER 3

Conditions

'The Works', a 'model' factory for its age, led the way in the world of science and new industrial technology. Its praises were sung far and wide by those who came to visit (but did not stay to work). George Measom, publisher and philanthropist, declared in his *Illustrated Guide to the Great Western Railway* published in 1852: 'Swindon, all-important Swindon; who that knows aught of railways, or railway travelling, has not heard of Swindon's worldwide reputation … for the vastness of its workshops and engine-depot.' The Works was a place created for engines (and later rolling stock) and machines, *not* for the men who worked there. It was first and foremost a place for work. It did not account for the 'comfort needs' of its workers. Conditions were horrendous and remained so for well over a hundred years. The Works' reputation in respect of accidents was legendary, especially in its earliest days – 'there is more that one accident on average per week for which Mr Rae is sent to attend the Works, or the man is *carried* to him,' Gooch wrote in his letter to the Board when seeking to formally engage the doctor for the Works and relieve the men 'from the cost of numerous accidents'. Such was the situation in November 1874 that serious concerns were raised in the local paper and Loco Works' Manager Samuel Carlton was stung into writing 'To All Foremen':

> Several cases have recently occurred in the Factory without the accident being reported to this office. The Company has been censured in the Daily Paper for their neglect in this matter. I must beg to call the particular attention of all Foremen to the importance of reporting all accidents in which the person injured is unable to return to his work by nine o'clock the following day. I trust this matter will be strictly carried out in the future.

Despite its poor reputation it is not to say that the GWR (and then BR) did nothing to ameliorate this situation – they did – but obviously it was not enough, and then, in later BR days, possibly too much! The Works Annual Report for 1965, when wages grade staff stood at 4,702, states that there were 269 accidents, of which 131 resulted in absence from duty, 116 entailing an absence of more than three days and so were reported to HM Inspector of Factories, but there were no fatal accidents. What is interesting to note in this same report is, at a time of increasing Health and Safety, the large number of consultations at the Works'

Surgeries – 2,525 'patients' made 6,702 attendances on the Loco side, whilst 1,245 'patients' made 2,877 attendances at the C & W Casualty Clinic. Today, in these days of insanely stringent Health and Safety Regulations, much of the work carried out inside the factory would be prohibited, or carry such restrictions that they would be almost impossible to meet, so it is hard for us to truly appreciate the reality of the conditions. One can find little in official company records that reflect the true nature of the working environment; to do that one has to look at the consequence of the conditions in reports of accidents, in articles and editorials in local newspapers, personal writings and oral testimony.

In September 1866 *The Swindon Advertiser* remarked: 'In the 1850s there was some comment on the large number of accidents that happened, some were obviously due to the carelessness of the workmen, but more to bad working conditions'. Three years later on 8 March 1869 under the heading: FRIGHTFUL ACCIDENT IN THE GWR NEW CARRIAGE WORKS AT SWINDON the paper reports: 'A shocking and fateful accident occurred on Wednesday last to a lad named William Hall, a labourer employed in the New Carriage Works in course of construction.' It told that William was learning to work a sawing machine but that morning

Many men and boys lost their lives in the Works. Roberts Hanks, 'a workman in the factory for twenty-nine years', was 'accidentally killed' on 11 September 1866, aged seventy-one years, and was buried in St Mark's graveyard.

'the machine was stopped so he wandered about the workshop in quest of something to do …
he went into the cellar where the shafting was being erected.'

At the inquest into his death held at the Cricketers Arms Inn, a Mr George Ripley, an
engineer down from Rochdale to assist in the erecting of the machinery in the workshops,
reported: 'I was in the cellar where the shafts were being erected under the floor of the saw
mills. The deceased had been assisting me to remove some concrete. I turned round to go to
the vice to get some chisels when I heard a faint scream.'

William Brown, a labourer in the C& W and 'mate' to Ripley, was also present at the time.
He believed that Hall:

> must have been playing with the belt and then got his arm entangled which drew him over
> the shaft. I heard a very peculiar scream and on looking round saw the deceased on the shaft. I
> ran directly to help Ripley throw the strap off to stop the shaft. As soon as the shaft slackened
> speed the deceased fell to the ground. I picked him up and found that he breathed once or
> twice and then died.

G.M. Swinhoe, the then surgeon and medical attendant to GWR workers, told the inquest: 'I
examined the body of the deceased. His left leg was entirely torn from the body. The left side of
the pelvis [was] fearfully lacerated. There were compound fractures of each forearm, and several
contusions about the head. His death resulted from these injuries.'

Whilst it is generally recognised and accepted that during the GWR era the Works was
always a dangerous place with a somewhat 'cavalier' attitude to workmen's safety, it would
appear that in this instance the GWR had attempted some sort of safety precautions as Samuel
Waits, a mechanic in the Works, also present at the time of the accident, explained to the Jury
that he had been: 'sent over to the new Carriage Works with instructions to fence in all the
straps and dangerous machinery that is being erected there.' A juryman also supports the view
that thought and purpose had been given to matters of safety. He stated that: 'the machinery
in these shops is fixed on a much better principle than in other places as all the shafting is
under the floors to avoid accidents of this kind.' The jury returned a verdict that the deceased
was 'accidentally killed through incautiously taking hold of a loose belt and being drawn over
the shafting.'

A few years later in 1871 another article in the paper regarding a 'Visit to the Carriage Works'
makes reference to this accident. Explaining how the massive machinery in the shop is kept
working and unclogged by the disposing of sawdust and shavings 'into the chamber below', the
article goes on to inform the reader that it was:

> down here that the first, and we believe up to the present, the only serious accident in the
> new Carriage Works took place. It is one of those strange and mysterious looking places …
> a region of straps and shafting and driving wheels … a wilderness of confusion and driving
> skeins. No wonder that the poor young countryman, on going down there, very quickly lost
> his head, and that the shafting and the straps took his body and played with it like a football.

Sixty years later in the 1930s and Hugh Freebury remembers his father, Harry, talking
of similarly appalling deaths: 'one poor fellow who had been caught up in a huge planeing

machine and killed instantly and another who was nearly decapitated when sitting astride his grinding machine and the grindstone burst. The poor fellow's brain were splashed over the wall and nobody knew what to do.'

Whilst some men lost their lives in the factory, others lost their limbs. In his history of the GWR Medical Fund Society, Bernard Darwin writes of what he calls 'a relatively small event' in 1878 when 'an unfortunate man called Harris was run over by a train and had to have his legs cut off.' Fortunately for Harris he was a member of the Society who 'provided him with a pair of legs having sockets, which were something of a novelty.' These, made in the Works, were probably the first ones to be so. Despite the circumstances one cannot help but admire the creative innovation to which the technical expertise of the engineer and the skill of the carpenter craftsman are put. Not content to offer 'a peg-leg', they created a wooden limb with 'sockets' that offered more flexibility. So many men lost limbs working on the GWR system that the Company introduced a designated 'artificial limb' shop into the Works, with 'work carried out between three departments, which have to do with the substances involved,

The first artificial limb recorded as being produced for a man in the Works, a Medical Fund Society member, was in 1878. A GWR *Magazine* article (1940) tells of the intricacies involved in producing 'a model of a human hand fashioned from willow ... with a combination of little devices, knuckle joints and hidden springs that allow the thumb and finger to execute normal movements.' During the 1950s a 'rehabilitation' shop was also introduced for workmen recovering from injury. They worked on specially modified machines which produced components for actual use in the factory.

B.2. SHOP. G.W.R. WORKS

William Hooper, Swindon's famous photographer of the nineteenth century, some of whose photographs appear in this book, worked in B Shed between 1882 and 1890. B Shed was one of the first workshops to be built by Brunel in 1842. It was an impressive place not least because of the giant traverser that ran the length of the shop. William's unfortunate accident involved this impressive traverser, the consequence of which was he had to have his leg amputated, after which he never regained full strength. He was put on light duties but with concerns over his safety he ended up leaving the Works. Happily for William, and fortunately for those interested in historical photographs, his previous hobby of photography turned into a full-time commercial profession. This is one of his. (Paul Williams' Hooper Collection)

wood, leather and metal.' Special consideration was given to the interests of the individuals so that sports people had legs of beech wood rather than the customary willow and others were given hands that had adaptations for holding pens to write. By the 1930s some 4,000 limbs had been issued. Two of the recipients were renowned photographer William Hooper who lost his leg as a result of an accident with the impressive traverser in B Shed in 1886, and, decades later, Graham Marchmant's grandfather, Charles Wallace Marchment, who started in the early 1900s in the Rolling Mills and had his accident in the 1930s. Graham tells: 'He lost his leg in there. He stood on a nail that was in a piece of wood. His wound went gangrene and he had to have his leg amputated just below the knee in the GWR hospital. That finished him. He never went back to his proper work.' John Lee who came down from London and into the Works in 1960 witnessed a serious accident to his chargeman Reggie Page in 1964. John was driving the biggest gantry in the Works in the Points & Crossing section of the Railyard. Reggie, trying to speed things up, pushed the truck down the line to him, but then had to go for the brake on the wagon – he missed, and it ran over his two feet. Despite his protective metal-capped shoes he lost all his toes. As an NUR representative John visited Reggie in hospital. He recalls Reggie bravely joking: 'I have to learn to walk again, but now I can wear any size shoes.'

Other aspects of danger for the men were in respect of ears and eyes – hearing and sight. Many of the shops in the Works were indescribably noisy places; layer upon layer of sound so that the men were enveloped by noise. It is a wonder that it is only hearing loss they suffered and not brain damage too! Rivetting was one of the earliest types of job in the Works. In 1891 journalist A.H. Malan had 'A Look Round Swindon Works' and wrote of the experiences in the *English Illustrated Magazine*:

> Noise, indeed, there is more or less everywhere throughout this busy hive, but the finest effects of genuine ear-splitting clatter are naturally met with in the riveting shops. Hydraulic riveters … do all the work within their reach, just giving one noiseless 'squelch' with their great crab-like callipers upon the red-hot iron… But where those silent workers cannot operate, for lack of space or other reason, there *human* riveters are in all their glory, showing their appreciation of the pandemonium they create, by performing merry ratatans with their hammers at every moment of waiting. It is sad to think that these men seem all doomed to be deaf, but on the whole this appears to be a merciful dispensation than if they were doomed to retain the faculty of hearing unimpaired.

Rivetting originally required a gang of at least three. The 'rivet-heater', later known as the 'rivet-hotter' or 'hotter-upper,' one of the lowliest jobs in the Works, was usually a young lad not yet started out on his apprenticeship, although apprentices did do this work too, and also, during the Second World War, conscripted young girls and women. It was the rivet-hotter's job to each day start a small coke fire which had then to be maintained at a certain heat by using bellows and careful feeding of extra coke. They had to collect the required rivets, sort them in order of size wanted, then heat the rivets until they were almost white hot, making sure not to overheat and so burn them to cinders; then once at the required temperature the rivet had to be picked up with tongs and tossed to 'the holder-upper'.

Hugh Freebury hated his time rivet-hotting in the 1930s, especially 'the long frequent trek up the yard for the binful of coke, the acid fumes from the forge and the all-pervading dust in my hair and down my collar', as well as the sheer boredom of it. 'Once you had mastered the practice of heating rivets to the satisfaction of your mates there was no challenge whatsoever. Sometimes one would come back because it had become 'nobbled' where I'd burnt it trying to do the job too well,' but for Hugh, that was as exciting as it got. Mrs E.P., a Second World War recruit, however, much preferred it to nut-scragging. 'It was a hard job,' she said, 'especially in the summer 'cos it got so hot … but you just had to keep going. We wore overalls and a heavy leather apron for protection.'

The 'catcher' was known as the 'holder-upper' (this was another job passed onto women in the Second World War) whose first task was to make sure to catch the burning hot rivet in a metal cup before picking it up with tongs and pushing it through the metal plate. Once there it had to be held firmly in position. This was done with a special large hammer, using the handle of the hammer as a lever to push the head of the hammer against the head of the rivet while the striker rained down a series of heavy blows flattening the rivet into place. Remember that this was while he/she stood *inside* the boiler. Pat Sullivan's grandfather was a holder-upper. It horrifies him to think of the dreadful conditions his relative worked in.

On his marriage certificate my grandfather's trade is a boilermaker's holder-upper and my great-grandfather, I think, was a boiler maker as well. In the boiler the rivets go from the inside out, same as bolts on a tender. The rivet-hotter would chuck a bolt up into the firebox, my grandfather would catch it with tongs, push it in and hold it with a big hammer against the back of it while the riveter riveted it from the outside. The boiler was like a speaker, the noise just echoed inside it. It's hard to believe. Now they wouldn't dream of doing it. They'd have to wear so much protection to even allow it. A friend of mine said there were three sorts of boiler maker – some were deaf, some were daft, and some were both! When you think about the work they were doing – the noise and everything – well I can relate to that. They couldn't hear each other talk of course. They'd stand nose to nose and shout and still couldn't hear each other, so everyone was lip reading and had bits of cotton waste stuck in their ears and things like that.

Albert John 'Jackie' Pinnegar (left), 'holder-upper' in the V Boiler Shop with his 'mate', c.1948. His job was to hold his hammer against the red-hot rivet from inside the engines' boiler while it was being riveted with a pnuematic rivetting gun from the outside. Many of these men became 'stone deaf' from the incessant noise; all suffered some degree of hearing loss and/or ringing in the ears.

The third and last member of the team was the 'striker' armed, in the earliest days, before hydraulic rivet guns, with only a sledgehammer, but in later years with both. While rivet-hotters would come and go as boys progressed through their apprenticeship, the striker and holder-upper were the men who stayed, some of the many workers in the Works who were doomed to deafness.

Boilermakers were a notable group of men destined for deafness and the possibility of losing an eye! The boilermaker's tools of his trade – the hammer and chisel – were said to be 'his best friends' but they were also his 'worse enemy' from the 'chips' they let fly, often being the cause of him losing an eye or suffering sight damage. Hugh Freebury recalls: 'Several times in my boyhood I can remember Father coming home and saying, "Nother boilermaker rushed up to London. They think he'll lose his eye".'
(Paul Williams' Hooper Collection)

A foundry workman, pouring molten metal, wears protective gloves and hated 'panda' glasses. Jack Fleetwood worked in the foundries from 1938 and remembers:

> Health and Safety was very poor until the 1960s. We did get issued with protective goggles, all metal with window glass in the lens, but if you dropped them they would shatter and they gave you hot red rings like 'panda-eyes' and 'styes' on your eyelids which were very painful.

Another incredibly noisy 'inside the boiler' job was working as a fitter. Ernie Fischer's father, Frederick J. Fischer, had been a boilermaker and had warned him about the tremendous noise, so Ernie was half expecting it when he started as a fitter doing the internals of the boiler in the 1950s, but even so he was taken aback:

> I worked inside the boiler a lot of the time and they would be hammering outside. All our work was hand work, hammer and chisel. We didn't use the guns. If they were cutting the pipes off, it was all done by hand. To start with the noise was awful. It was terrific, but I got used to it in time. Oh, yeah, it affects your hearing bad.

Mike White, who spent sometime working inside the boilers, suffers from severe hearing loss in both ears as well as tinnitus, which began when he was just twenty years old. Long after Nationalisation 'noise pollution' was still a problem and in the 1970s when people were more aware of their 'rights' Brian Maddicks claimed and received £2,000 compensation for hearing loss from the effects of being constantly beside the engine 'Test beds' waiting for engines to come off on to the trailers on which he worked.

Eye hazards were common in almost all the workshops. Jack Fleetwood had a terrifying experience in the foundry in the 1950s:

I had a 'near-miss' when skimming back the scum off a pot of molten metal when the chap
pouring spilt some. There was a bang and I closed my eyes instinctively. I was not wearing
goggles. Anyway I opened my eyes and found that only one would open. I dashed over to the
wall where there was a bit of broken mirror, and to my relief it was just a piece of metal had
stuck the lids together.

One of the ways the GWR and later BR sought to lessen the physical damage and trauma
of accidents was through the 'first-aider'. It is believed that first-aiders began to appear
in the Works in the 1880s; before this time it was very much 'wait-for-the-doctor' or

Sawmill No.2, Bristol Street, c.1880. Roy Blackford remembers that 'eye problems' occurred regularly
on the C & W side too. To combat this most men carried their own self-made 'eye-loop' to run over
the eye and lift out the offending material. This was simply a little stick with a small loop of soft
bristle-type material such as cat-gut, which they would keep in a 'case', i.e. a stick of wood with a hole
bored through the middle with a little cap on the end, ready in their pockets. It became an unofficial 'tool
of the trade'!

'do-the-best-you-can-yourselves'. Whilst initially viewed with some scepticism and suspicion – how could an ordinary bloke like themselves know proper medical stuff? – these men, and later women too, through the St John's Ambulance movement, grew to be a major and well-respected presence in the Works. In order to maintain interest and keep standards high, annual ambulance competitions were introduced into the Works in 1900 when William Dean presented the Swindon Ambulance Committee with a silver cup for this purpose. To gain a St John's Certificate one had to attend lectures, practice classes and competitions as well as carry out the practical application on those who needed it under supervision. As well as the respect of one's peers, being a first-aider carried additional perks. An additional free pass for oneself and immediate family was granted to each fully employed member who passed the examination. After passing fifteen annual examinations one got an extra one-day's paid holiday, and after thirty annual examinations two days extra paid holiday. Many workers have memories of having to resort to 'the first-aider'. Mrs Ada Werrel was one:

> I had the top fly off the machine once; I put my hand up to protect my face, the top chipped my thumb and it began bleeding badly. I went over to the Ambulance man on the side and he had his ambulance box. When I went back to my machine I was a bit white with shock and Mr Bill Bloomfield, my chargeman, said 'just go outside and have a little sit'. He helped me outside. When I came back in the men gave me a little whistle.

Roy Blackford remembers that when grit got right up under the eye-lid, 'The Ambulance man would turn it back over itself and then we would use the eye-loop.'

Over the years whilst the Works was continuously improved and upgraded in terms of work 'production', working 'conditions' did not keep apace. If we compare the experiences of Alfred Williams at the turn of the twentieth century to those of Jack Hayward in the second half of that century, it would appear that very little had changed at all. Williams describes the conditions of the Works in the early 1900s in such graphic detail one cannot fail to feel the discomfort:

> the dense smoke and fumes from the oil forges, and the thick sharp dust and ashes from the coke fires … the tremendous noise of the hammers and machinery and the priming of the boilers have a most injurious effect upon the body as well as the nervous system … it is all intensely painful and wearisome to the workmen … a great number of accidents are due directly or indirectly to the unhealthy air about the place … the heat is far more painful to endure … especially in close and stuffy shed … it will be impossible for the workmen to maintain any degree of strength or vigour … the temperature in front of the furnaces will be considerably over 100 degrees and when the air is stagnant and thick and heavy with nauseous smoke and fumes … it is positively tortuous … the perspiration seems to be drawn from your bones…

Jack Hayward, who entered the Works as a shop clerk over forty years later, writes of very similar conditions in 1956:

'Class of 1898.' St John's Ambulance Association, introduced into the Works around the 1880s, played a significant role thereafter. A 1936 GWR census of 'Ambulance Workers' identified that of the 11,861 employed in Swindon Works and offices, 385 were qualified. A year later a *Magazine* article informed that there were 103 dressing stations within the Works, one or more in every shop, and some 500 men then with a St John's certificate.

The memories of my first day on 16 January 1956 remain with me to this day. It was such a cultural and physical shock. I reported to the Staff Office wearing my best suit, as you would as an office worker, and was met by the Chief Clerk, Bert Woolford, of the F1 Blacksmith Shop office where I was to work. I followed him across what was called the G shop yard to the entrance of the Spring Shop and went through huge double doors. I was appalled by the scenes on the other side; it was as if I had gone back into history by a hundred years. The air was filled with fumes from the many coke fires used by the blacksmiths, mixed in was a pall of fine dust rising from the ash floor, which clung to the walls like a sprinkling of black snow, the ash was to prevent the men from slipping while working with red hot metal and every two or three hours the floor would be hosed down to lay the dust.

   As I walked down the shop my mind reeled. There were all these muscular men looking very Dickensian. They had sort of worsted woollen trousers on, these great big heavy canvas aprons and white shirts with their sleeves rolled up and no collar and I thought 'blooming heck'. Past the Spring shop furnaces we approached a huge circular saw in the middle of the shop. A blacksmith with the help of two of his mates carried a large billet of red hot metal from the fire between them, and with the aid of their tongs placed it under the saw.

As I drew level I stepped into a blaze of sparks that shot right up into the roof and showered down on to me from every angle, and to me, this was the most terrifying reception imaginable. As I passed through this fiery rain, I expected to see the worse for my best suit, at least a few singe marks but there was not a mark on me, later I learned that the sparks were harmless. We continued on our way down the shop accompanied by the din of pounding steam hammers and the high-pitched scream of this huge saw cutting through hot metal as easy as a hot knife cuts through butter. You couldn't hear anything except banging. My heart sank, and my mood matched the gloom that surrounded me. I thought, 'I'm not going to enjoy this'.

By the time I reached home that lunch time, my mind was made up, never to go back to that place. My mother listened to my story, she knew what I was trying to describe, my parents were of the generation that had grown up and worked their whole lives under these conditions. I was persuaded to give it more time, after all my father had worked there as too did uncle Wally and uncle Ivor.

To say toilet facilities in the Works were basic and primitive is putting it politely. Alongside this was the lack of dignity that accompanied a visit to use them. Use of the toilets was timed. One had to shout out your check number to the attendant as you went in so the time could

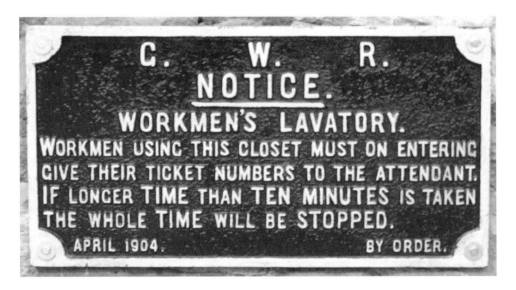

Dusty Durrant recalls the toilets during his apprenticeship in the 1940s:

In the yard between R and G Shops, dating from the original works, was a very primitive form of lavatory having a row of cubicles whose seat was placed over an open drain through which water flowed continuously. The prank here was to occupy the up-stream cubicle early and when several lower down were comfortably occupied by workmen having their early morning session … a crumpled up newspaper would be ignited and floated down the water stream, singeing several bottoms on route. One had to flee rapidly before the enraged owners could dress and pursue.

be noted, ensuring you did not overstay your ten minutes allowed and if you did, you would be reported to the foreman. Lack of privacy was yet another indignity as the toilet doors not only didn't have locks but also had a 5-6in-diameter hole in them through which the attendant could check if anyone was indulging in reading the paper or catching up on the racing results (a favourite preoccupation in the Works). The men would try to overcome this 'spying' by taking off their slop jackets and pushing them into the hole, although it was not unknown for them to be poked out again! When smoking was forbidden, prior to 1939, woe betide any man foolish enough to be caught smoking in the toilet, as R. Alder recalls of the early 1930s: 'the toilet attendant would kick the door open and drag you out with your trousers round your ankles and a report was sent to your foreman. A second report meant you were sent home for a day without pay.'

Jack Hayward vividly remembers the indignity of these 'shared' toilet facilities that left a marked impression on him:

> The cubicles were like nothing I had ever seen or want to see again, and this awful visit was sufficient to dissuade me from making a second visit – ever, even in the most dire of emergencies. The short wooden door had a large gap at the bottom, which one could say was acceptable, but what I found to be most disquieting was the very large circular hole cut in the centre of each door, so that while sitting in a contemplative manner one's head and shoulders were in full view of passers-by much as though you were appearing on a television screen. Yet another feature that I found positively alarming was that instead of the usual pedestal arrangement one is accustomed to or even a double hole, much favoured by country dwellers at the time, we had a low wall upon which to sit with a water trough flowing behind and into the next cubicle.

Such primitive facilities were the reason that Collet, then Locomotive Works Manager, baulked (understandably) at the thought of women in the Works during the First World War. Whilst women had been 'Inside' in the C & W's French Polishing and Trimming Shops since 1874, their shops and facilities there were 'built' especially for them and were kept altogether separate. During the First World War women had to be introduced into the factory proper to help with the war effort. It then became absolutely necessary to provide suitable toilet arrangements. An official drawing identified as 'lavatory accommodation for women Loco Works, Swindon' dated October 1916 and written up as 'adopted', shows that, happily for the women, toilet and canteen accommodation was instigated for female employees in the old K Shop, which was the old coppersmith's shop. Even in 1966 men's workshop toilet facilities were still very poor as remarked on by a union representative visiting the Works in August that year. The *Wiltshire Gazette & Herald* carried headlines stating: 'Conditions in BR Works are criticised':

> Conditions in Swindon railway works came in for strong criticism from a trade unionist on Wednesday. An Amalgamated Engineering Union representative, Mr J Chequer, at Swindon Trades Council told members: 'I am no British Rail employee, but last week I visited the Works, the antiquated washing facilities and toilets appalled me. If the British Transport Commission were private individuals they would be jailed.

In 1962, not far short of half a century after Alfred Williams' book, during the fading days of steam but with dieselisation already in the workshops, Jack Hayward went into the Chair Foundry as pictured above:

I reported to the J1 Iron Foundry shop office. Although my desk was in the Iron Foundry office my work took me into the J2 Chair Foundry. Before taking this new post I had no idea what a rail chair was, it looked nothing like the things we sit on but was an iron casting made in their thousands and their function was to fix railway lines to the sleepers. Heinz, the man whose job I was taking over, gave me a tour of my new territory. It shook me to the core, I was appalled by the filthy conditions, and my complaints against the Blacksmith Shop paled into insignificance compared with the scenes that now attacked my senses.

The floor was fabricated from steel boilerplates on which were row upon row of moulding boxes filling the entire floor of the foundry. At the west corner of the foundry was the cupola where the cast iron was produced and from where the men would fill their ladles (which were cast iron cauldrons on two wheels with a long shaft and a handle) with molten iron and literally run down the shop making the pour as they went, molten iron would slop over the edge of the ladle, spitting and crackling as it hit the iron floor before setting like ball bearings. The pour had to be made before the temperature of the molten iron dropped to a certain level, as that would produce a faulty casting. The hectic activity in the foundry at this time made it a potentially dangerous place to be, especially with occurrence of tiny ball bearings on the plated floor, which created a particular hazard to the runners with their ladles of molten iron.

As the pour was being made so the boxes released a cloud of grey smoke accompanied by a most obnoxious acrid stench that not only filled the foundry but also permeated the air up to half a mile away, and with the Foundry building being so close to Rodbourne Road people in the area constantly complained of the filth blowing down from the cupola's chimney onto them. Men were working in this disgusting environment day and night and as the pour progressed the polluted atmosphere became so thick with this sulphurous smoke that it was literally impossible to see the opposite side of the foundry.

After the casting had been allowed to set the pegs holding the boxes together would be knocked out and the casting separated from the dry sand polluting the air with evil-smelling dust. At best the environment could be described as grimy, but without a doubt it was not a healthy one. The description of my new working abode from then on became 'Hell's Kitchen'.

This visit must have done the trick because these toilets were refurbished and updated at great cost, only to be demolished a few years later! Jack Fleetwood recalls that washing facilities where he worked in the Brass Foundry were very primitive too, this where the men were handling horse manure to mix in with the sand to make the right consistency for the moulds. 'When you wanted to wash your hands you had a dirty concrete trough – pigs ate out of cleaner ones – and a few dirty thin towels. Soap was what was called 'sand soap' – more sand than soap! We must have had some tough skin otherwise we would all have been down with some disease or other.' The 1958 Annual Report of CM & EE's department states under 'Welfare' that 'a large scheme in connection with washing and messing facilities in the Iron Foundry has been agreed in principle,' but it wasn't until the 1960s that conditions actually physically improved.

'Hot-shops' by their very nature were dangerous places. Working with volatile hot metals with possibilities for explosions was a serious hazard for the men. Albert Dawes, a cylinder moulder, worked on the cylinder gang in such a shop – the Iron Foundry. Albert had good memories of working on many of GWR's 'classic' engines – Kings and Castles – but bad memories of his accident: 'I tripped and lost my balance, falling into a ladle of red-hot metal, but a pal grabbed me and prevented a worse catastrophe. As it was I badly burned my elbow and was off work for weeks before the Works' Doctor, Roddy Swinhoe, gave me the all-clear'.

These women are welding wagon fittings in 21a Shop C & W side during the Second World War. The women worked in the same poor conditions with the men. Mrs Peggy Thompson (*née* Eggleton) went into the Works in 1942 aged eighteen and was moved between shops for the next twelve years. She worked on the machines in R Shop; she did bomb shell turning in 15 Shop; rivet hotting in 13 Shop, and finally the lighter work of sorting out the screws in the Polishing Shop after she became pregnant. She left in 1954, one of the few women to have stayed on after the war ended. Despite it being 'dirty and noisy' she would have loved to have stayed longer.

Whilst the men became habituated and accepting of the harsh conditions so that they no longer impacted on their consciousness, women entering the workshops during the Second World War were horrified. Mrs Phyllis Saunders who worked in the Blacksmith's Shop vividly remembered:

It was a terrible place to have to work. It was filthy. There was not much air. There was a few windows at the top, almost up at the roof. They were seldom opened because they were a job to get to, but we did open them at times because the walls and everything got so filthy. It got so hot with all those open fires. I picked up a bad throat, just off diphtheria. I think it was all the dirt probably. I had some time off and the doctor treated it with Penicillin – twice!

Mrs Ada Werrell recalls how angry she and the other women in AM Shop felt:

I went to AM Shop. That was a big shop, not at all nice. I was glad my husband didn't work in there. It was like the blackhole of Calcutta. It was a mass of belts, no electric motors then, and all oil on the floor. We had no rest rooms, we had a chair by our machine and we slung our coats across that and put our things there. There was only a urn on a stand and the men

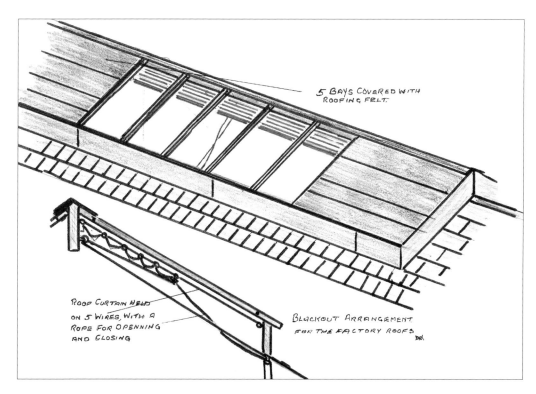

Conditions in the Works were exacerbated by 'the blackout' during the Second World War. Bill Maynard's sketch shows the arrangements for the factory roofs. As a member of the Maintenance Gang in the Loco D Shop, it was part of Bill's job to remove all of the glass panels, except for the middle five, from the roofs for storage until after the war and cover the roofs with black roofing felt. The five remaining glass panels in each workshop had to be fitted with roof curtains that could be closed from the shop floor by means of a wire. The curtains were made from a light blue material with eyelets inserted for the wires to be attached. The workshops affected covered an area of around 389 acres. Bill remembers that during the changeover period it was noticed that the stock of the curtain material kept in the shops had the mysterious habit of diminishing overnight without explanation, however it was also noticed that during this period of serious clothes rationing there appeared to be a high proportion of the Swindon male population walking about the town in light blue suits. Stripping the material off after the war gave 200 Works' 'volunteers' over nine successive weekends' overtime. Happy days!

would come with their cans for water for their tea. It was bad, no facilities, not fit for women to work in. It got on our nerves. Alright we'd been in factories before. I worked with men before, but we did have facilities, decent toilets. About six or eight of us walked out one day, we went down to the Labour Exchange, but we had to go back with our tails between our legs. We had no say then.

Many shops, like the Bolt Shop, had similar reputations, yet for some creatures they were places of refuge, a place to call 'home'. For whom? Cats. Nearly all the shops had cats as pets or regular visitors. Why? Because of the rats. The Works was heavily infested with them. Gordon Ing remembers them: 'I had to go up in the roof in the Stamping Shop, there was grease around the bearings, and there were rats as big as cats up in that roof'. Ask any woman who worked in the shops during the war period what their overriding memory of the Works is and they will almost always answer – 'rats'. Mrs Enid Saunders especially remembers them in the Tube Shop 'running up and down in the tubes'. The women remember them particularly well as the men thought it a great joke to bang the pipes and make the rats squeak and scurry about, making the women squeak and scurry about too! In an effort to keep down the rats, the cats were not just tolerated but encouraged to stay. 'Mind the cat' was a phrase often heard shouted. The only place they would not stay was in the foundries, which the men believe was because of the heavy fumes in there.

For most the C & W side conjures up a cleaner, healthier environment, but this was not so of all shops there as Jim Rogers knows too well:

On 1 November 1939 I went 'Inside'. My first job was in the C & W Stamping House, 18 Shop. Dreadful it was. The first impression was that it was very dirty, very noisy and very dark. The lighting was gas lighting, not very bright and it seemed all you could see was the fire of the furnaces. There were furnaces, presses and hammers. I was taken down the shop by the under-chargeman Stan Bown. There was this little space between two cupboards. He sat me down on an old coach seat spring and said 'You sit in there and I'll come and fetch you when we need you.' He was a really nice man, he was always singing hymns at work and used to preach at weekend. We called him Pastor Bown.

Jim Osman, who started as a fitter/turner apprentice on the carriage side in 1950, also spent some time in the Stamping Shop. He agrees 'It was a really terrible place to work in, full of clouds of smoke, the smell of oil, but I was pleased I did it. It was a real experience to see the amazing work that was done in there.' Later when working on maintenance Jim found that 'when we had to go up into the roof in there, we'd put the ladder against the wall and clouds of dust and dirt would come down. Filthy it was. We looked like a miner after working up there.' Jim's grandfather, Richard Osman, spent forty years in the Works starting in 1894. He worked for many years in the Grinding House in the Machine Shop on the C & W side. Richard's retirement in 1934 was reported by the local paper stating that Richard was known as the 'father of the Grinding House' or the 'grand old man'. His age was obviously exceptional in this shop as it was also reported that he had the special distinction of being the first person in the Grinding House to reach retirement age. There was no extraction in the shop then and no masks provided, so grinders, balanced on their wooden planks, swaying to and fro over the grind stones, would inhale the dust and would later suffer from respiratory and digestive problems.

Not all work was done inside a shop or shed. Some had to be done outside and conditions could be just as tough as Roy Blackford discovered:

I went over to a place nicknamed 'Klondyke', this was where the repairs were done over by Rodbourne Rec., 24 Shop, the other side of the Gloucester Line. I went over there on my seventeenth birthday. I always remember it, 1 February 1947, and it was snowing hard. I'd heard tales from the lads who'd been and come back, and they were right, it was just like Klondyke. If you've ever seen pictures of the old Gold Rush, that's more or less how it was. All the old coaches were dotted around in the sidings, there were big oil drums, forty gallon drums with timber burning trying to keep us warm. A lot of the lads over there in '47 had just come back out of the Forces. They were getting about in RAF or Army greatcoats, even Navy ones. It was freezing. That winter, I suppose, went down as one of the hardest ever. I still remember it. We were working outside. I mean it wouldn't be tolerated now. There was

Working outside on old steam freight locomotives during the 1960s was just as dirty and challenging as working in some shops. These locos were cut up and the steel smelted down for use in building new diesel engines.

no steam heating. I think eventually there was one road that had the steam heating on and sometimes the shunter would forget about the heating, they'd come over with the shunting engine and go away and drag all the steam joints out of the ground and there'd be a jet of steam going up and you'd be freezing cold.

Whilst the GWR would ensure that adequate facilities and the best possible equipment was available for production, they regarded other expenditure, all of which would have to be explained to their shareholders, unnecessary, and would not spend the pennies on such unless coerced into doing so. Against this seeming Scrooge-like attitude it has to be remembered that during virtually the whole of its existence the Works was up against the constant need for GWR to exact strict and often severe economies. Even after Nationalisation in the early post-Second World War years there was little cash available for 'personal comfort' and only later, when 'outside' people came and commented, and Health and Safety requirements became more rigorous, did it really impact on those who had become accustomed to

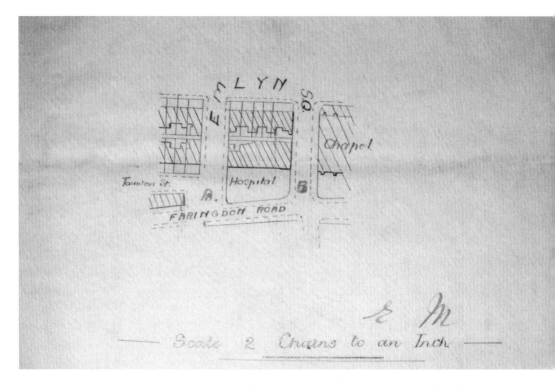

One option of obtaining breakfast food available to the men came through the services of a Mrs May Ellen who resided at 207 Rodbourne Road. A contract dated 21 February 1908 between the GWR and Mrs Ellen shows that for the sum of 'ten pound and ten shillings per annum' she was granted licence to: 'stand with two portable stalls (one large and the other small) at the points shown A and B on the map for the sale of Tea Coffee Bread and Butter and Cake in Emlyn Square Swindon, between the hours of 5 am and 9 am.' Mrs Ellen was required to conduct her business 'in a quiet and orderly manner and to the satisfaction of the Company and their officers'.

It took a long time for the GWR to provide an on-site canteen facility. The first was in London Street in 1878. Gradually, over the decades, there were many 'mess-rooms' and 'dining-halls' introduced on both sides of the Works. At times these were not only places of nourishment, but also places of entertainment, as during the 1940s when Wednesday concerts were introduced during the dinner break. (David Hyde Collection)

them. For many decades what the men did to quell their hunger and thirst when they were officially not working, well that was up to them. The only official 'break' was for the middle of the day period, any other eating or drinking was done 'on the sly', behind the foreman's back. Official circulars show that in the early years the workmen were not allowed to stay in the shops or sheds during meal breaks and that they were threatened with dire penalties if they did. A Circular dated January 1867 gives 'Caution to Workmen' and states 'men often remain in the Works at meal hours for a longer time after the ringing of the Bell than is necessary. I have to caution them that in future all persons found … after 6 minutes from the Bell ringing, will be reported to me and I shall take steps to prevent them so offending again.' For those who lived locally the tradition of dashing home for a cooked meal at dinner (lunch) time became established while Rule 10 (1875) stipulates that: 'mess rooms are provided for those who live at a distance.' These were probably just 'housing' facilities for the men whilst they ate their own food as in 1878 a small article in Astills' *Swindon Local Guide* tells that a 'newly erected Dining Room for the employees … occupies the lower portion of the large building fronting London Street. Rows of tables are arranged on each side capable of seating

450 persons.' It goes on to say:'It is presumed that the Company contemplate some provision in the shape of cooking apparatus which will render this convenience very complete and be a boon for the men who reside at some distance.' Later, cooking apparatus was introduced and later still 'cooks' too.

Alongside this the GWR Coffee Tavern Co. offered coffee rooms around the Company's network 'at which men can obtain wholesome food and refreshments at reasonable prices, apart from the temptations connected with the public house.' New Swindon's Coffee house was set up at 1 High Street (now Emlyn Square) and proved so successful and popular that it expanded next door to No.2.[1] These coffee taverns gave good service until they became a casualty of the newly structured day as a result of the forty-seven-hour week agreement which came into practice on 1 January 1919 and the 'breakfast-break' was dropped.[2]

Lorna Dawes remembers her father using the London Road mess-room in later years and taking an egg with his name on, which he would hand in in return for a ticket and come the break it would be waiting ready cooked for him. Most times though, like many other workers, Lorna's father ate his sandwiches, especially during the unofficial breaks, in the foundry amidst the thick black sand. He would hold his sandwich with paper in an effort to keep the sand (and dirt) off the sandwiches. He had a billycan to make drinks and an ingenious little can, sold by the local ironmongers, which had two compartments with a lid at each end, one for the sugar and one for the tea leaves. The 'hot-shops' came in handy when cooking or heating up one's food. Mrs Pam Arthurs (*née* Pinnegar) who worked in F Shop after the war, remembers her first experience of this:'We went in a lunchtime and the blacksmiths were toasting their toast on the anvil. They did the same for us, when we was in there. Never just bread, always toast on the anvil. One blacksmith used to put a kipper inside the fire on the coals then get it out and eat it every bit, bones and all.' Eating amongst all these toxic fumes often lead to more ill health. Jack Fleetwood remembers two brothers who worked in the Brass Foundry were suspected of having contracted lead poisoning from eating in there all the time; although this was a hazard known of decades before and part of Rule 5 (1904) was 'any workman absent through lead poisoning must inform his Foreman'. After the latter-day discovery a mess room was provided and the foundry men were given an allowance of a pint of milk a day in order to counteract the effects of any possible poisoning.

Over the decades various canteen facilities were provided for both sides of the Works then in the late 1960s the integration of the C & W and Loco departments necessitated the construction of yet another Works dining hall seating up to 580. It was to become the focus of a small, historic, political activity as covered by the *Swindon Advertiser*:

Thursday 3 April 1969

Canteen Strike – Petticoat Revolution by Swindon BR Canteen Staff
Hundreds go hungry as 10 women strike

It has taken just 10 women to paralyse the workshop catering service
Protesting over cuts in the staff which has to serve 300 meals a day and they also
want an £2 increase to their pay of £6 15s for a 40 hour week. The women including assistant

cooks, canteen assistants and kiosk attendants are members of the Transport and General Workers Union, Canteen Manageress Mrs Evelyn Scott is not among the strikers.

Mr Allen Davey outlined their grievances – 'Four years ago there was a staff of 25 and it has now come down to 11. The strike was based upon objections to a staff cut of 50% during four years and the basic pay rate supplemented only by a 17s a week meal allowance which was considered insufficient'. He would be reporting to the regional secretary to have the strike declared official.

A British Rail spokesman said that the management had been unable to agree to the demands of the women for a substantial increase in their nationally-agreed rates of pay.

Three days later Mrs Muriel Frankland (shop steward), Mrs Glen West and Mrs Winifred Lester start picketing at the gates and lorries are diverted away. Mrs Frankland told the *Advertiser*: 'We have been very patient but now we are getting very annoyed. We are playing the same game as the management and we are prepared to go all the way.' Over the next few days all ten women took it in turns to continue to picket. Members of the public stopped and said

The 'historical', female, T & GWU CANTEEN STAFF OFFICIAL STRIKE, 1969. From left to right: Mrs Muriel Frankland (shop steward), Mrs Gwen West and Mrs Winifred Lester outside Rodborne Road entrance. Their placard proclaims: 'B.R. Canteen Slaves 3/4*d* per hour.'

how disgusted they were at the low wages the women were getting. Whilst the women had the Public's sympathy, it wasn't quite so clear that they had the men's. At a time when strikes were called 'at the drop of a hat', to quote one man, it was noticeable that no men downed tools to join the women in their protest, a point highlighted by the Papers and Mr Albert Davey, the TGWU district organiser: 'I am not terribly impressed by the attitude of the people on the gate who are trying to interfere with you stopping the transport. They are trying to take advantage of you because you are women.' On Friday 25 April the women are joined on the picket by one lone male, Mr Bill Wheeler, the TGWU convenor in the Works, who angrily declared: 'I am absolutely disgusted by the lack of support of my TGWU membership in the Works … I firmly believe that if the membership inside had come out with them, we would have got the other unions in there to support them'. It is not until the unions have declared their 'official' support that management agrees to negotiate. On 29 April the month-old strike ended. The women had settled for 21 shillings extra a week, back-dated for six weeks; they also kept their 17s-a-week meal allowance. It is reported that the women returned to work 'assured of their status as queens of the kitchen' where they could reign without 'interference from outside'. This was the only 'female' strike in the history of the Works.

One cannot write about the conditions that existed without mentioning the terrible legacy of these conditions – one that many who worked 'Inside' would like to forget as it casts a sombre shadow over a rich history. Mesothelioma is a type of lung cancer caused by inhaling asbestos fibres, but what became known locally as 'The Swindon Disease' was really a number of respiratory diseases linked to asbestos.

To the workers asbestos, introduced in the Works in the 1930s, was just another material they worked with. For decades no one knew its hidden horrors. Peter Withers who started in the Works in 1945 remembers: 'Down the Carriage side there was a big shop where there was loads of it. We would even push each other in it. Nobody knew see.' The workers just accepted the 'white powder' that got everywhere – even, unknowingly, in your lungs. Even its storehouse was given an affectionate name, 'the Fluff House'! For a lark apprentices, and men, would damp it, roll it into balls and throw it at each other or throw the balls up against the ceiling to make them fall down again like powdered snow. Whilst working in the F2 Shop Mrs Pam Arthurs found 'the asbestos fell out of the ceiling like snow. It was put round the pipes as lagging in the winter.' Later in the 1950s and '60s blue asbestos was introduced. Still no one thought of protection, protective clothing or protective procedures, because no one then knew of its lethal legacy. Men in the AV Boiler Shop who worked directly with the powder, mixing it with water to the required consistency for application to the boilers, were obviously at great risk, but all were vulnerable, as Mike White recollects:

> It was even worse when they brought the boilers back in for stripping down, because when they took off the cleating the hardened asbestos coating would fall off or had to be knocked off and it would rise up in the air like clouds of dust. Even men in the AM Shop, who hadn't even worked with it, died from it, as the clouds of dust would blow through into their shop and they would be breathing it in.

A SHOP 1935

'The white dust', i.e. asbestos, was introduced into the Works in the 1930s and used to coat locomotive boilers for fire protection and insulation. It was also used on pipes in the Works. For decades it was just part and parcel of the materials one worked with, even played with, and none suspected its deadly menace. Many men suffered severe health consequences, from both direct and indirect contact. Men in the AM Shop, here machining white metal parts of axleboxes, although not working with it, would breathe in the asbestos dust clouds that wafted through from AV Boiler Shop when the cleating was being knocked off the boilers, and many were severely affected.

It is not known for sure when the perils of using this product became known, what is for sure is that it was the cause of death or blighting of the later lives of large numbers of Swindon Works' railwaymen. Peter Withers worked on a gang that had several members who were so affected. Peter remembers when 'asbestos awareness' began to creep in: 'They built a new asbestos house so that when the units came in they had to go in there and be stripped off. The men had protective everything then, but by then the damage had already been done.' Peter also remembers the amount of new work that was generated by people's growing awareness of the problem and the response to deal with it:

In those days [1930s–60s] they would spray the black paint and then spray the asbestos on top of that. That gave it a coating on the inside of the panels. When the argument came about the asbestos, the engine drivers discovered that the fibres were coming up into the cabs in the diesels, so they refused to take them out. It was decided to take the fronts off and put new ones on without the asbestos.

It was a big business the changing. The multiple units would come in on Friday. Then it was all go. First the front was took off, then the body makers would put a new front on. They were finished off Sunday and would go out on the line 6 am Monday morning. We did one a weekend 'til it was all done.

The coming of diesel raised hopes of better conditions, but initially things remained much the same. John Mudge, who was the first coppersmith apprentice to be seconded over to diesels in 1959, found that despite having been told 'it'll be different, easy, clean white overalls, a chance to sit and play cards' it was, in reality, just as dirty and smelly as steam, in fact he found it more so. John remembers:

The conversion of the Works from steam to diesel brought about many changes. The Works then struggled with something of a 'split personality', exacerbated by the continuing return of steam locos for refurbishment and preservation, such as the LMS *Duchess of Hamilton,* above, stood alongside Western Class 52, built in the Works but here awaiting demolition (*c.*1970). Many saw the transformation as hope for a brighter future for the Works and its tradesmen … and for a goodly number of years this was so.

Nineteenth-century 'Age of Steam' Iron Foundry where dirt floors, hot fires, molten metals, toxic fumes, nauseous smells, even explosions, made it a most hazardous place. No wonder the Works' cats wouldn't stay there! This early photograph of the south bay, where small castings were made, shows foundry men preparing moulding boxes ready for the pour. Molten iron was brought along the walkway from the cupola at the far end of the foundry in crucibles on trolleys to make the pour. On the left is the shop office where the clerical staff, workshop inspectors and the foremen were accommodated.

The 600s that came in from North British were in a dreadful state, falling to bits and filthy. Dirt can be brushed off, but the oil drips! They would start off as a 5p then spread out into a 10p, then merge with other drips and become bigger still, then dry. Your overalls could stand up on their own. Horrible it was. My mum would say, 'What's that funny smell?' It was the oil. It used to get in your hair too. You couldn't get rid of that smell. Even later when we worked on the Maybachs there was that smell and the ground-in oil in your hands.

Later, with diesel designated refurbishment things did improve enormously as Roger Hayes remembers: 'In the early days of changing from steam to diesel there were still the dreadful conditions that had existed. Then there was a massive refurbishment in the 1960s that changed things to the cleaner environment requirement of diesels'. There were still health problems though. Now it was dermatitis, on hands and arms, creating real problems, despite the barrier cream issued for protection. Roger explains:

> When they were cleaning the diesels, the power units, the contaminated oil would get all over their hands. There are a lot of detergents in oil and they would get into the skin and irritate and inflame it. The lanolin cream treatment wasn't always helpful and some men had to be transferred off to other jobs; some even moved into clerical work because their skin would not recover.

As the Works physically contracted and the nature of the work changed, further extensive upgrades and refurbishments were carried out; as Health and Safety became more important, more protective clothing and equipment were provided; and as men and unions became more demanding of their rights, more safety measures were enforced, until, eventually, the Victorian Works had at last been brought up to date and ready to face the twenty-first century.

Changed times! The north bay of the Iron Foundry (now 9 Shop) in the 'Age of Diesel' showing how clean it was compared to its previous existence. Here we can see power units and transmission from various locomotives. Items at front right: two automatic gear boxes, two reconditioned AEC 1500hp diesel horizontal engines and second trailer is of crankshafts either cleaned or machined DMUs. (David Hyde Collection)

The AE (Erecting) Shop, during the1960s. Dieselisation was to change the railway scene forever which, eventually, brought dramatic physical changes to the workshops, particularly in respect of cleanliness. Immediate front is a D7000 series 'Hymech'. Made in the Works with a Maybach V16-cylinder engine (1,750bhp), it was used mainly for pulling freight. Behind this is the 'Western' series, which had two Maybach engines each developing 1,350bhp. D1031 *Western Rifleman* lines up in front of D1000 *Western Advocate*. All main line service would be pulled by these new locos.

Endnotes

1.   *Great Western Railway Magazine*, Vol.111, No.27, 1891, and Vol.V, 1893.
2.   Alan Peck, p.190. (See Bibliography)

CHAPTER 4

What is a Railwayman?

What is a railwayman? There are some that say that a railwayman is a man who has steam in his veins rather than blood! Such an answer illustrates that many perceive a railwayman to be someone special, someone 'apart', even someone of a past age. What is a Swindon Works' railwayman? Well, that's an altogether different question. Judging by the reputation they had both at home and abroad it would appear that they were almost a breed apart. 'He's come down from Swindon,' was a phrase used by those at the different depots and stations along the system both in GWR and BR times, as if Swindon, being symbolically 'on high', people from there could only 'come down' to other places and lesser mortals.

The elemental factors of being a railwayman are bound up in issues of skill and time. Talk to any railwayman and they will always talk of 'time' – doing my time', 'coming out of my time', putting in the time' – 'time' was a fundamental component of railwaymen's lives. It was the essence of what made a *real* railwayman. 'Putting in the time' started when they were just boys.

Railwaymen in Waiting

Boys were employed in the Works right from the beginning. The first list of workers employed there cites thirty-five boys. The boys employed 'Inside' would have been the sons of the workmen and clerks employed there, as well as lads who had abandoned agriculture in the hope of better wages and job prospects. We know that boys as young as twelve, and maybe even a little younger, were employed in the Works as the record of a fatal accident of one boy verifies. In 1862 William Morris wrote:

> The fearful death of a lad named Leech occurred in the Swindon Railway Works, in consequence of his entanglement in the driving straps connecting some powerful machinery. This lad, although but twelve years of age, had for sometime been engaged in the good work of earning his own livelihood by honest labour. He was a good lad and a great favourite with the men in the shop in which he worked.

Railwaymen and broad-gauge engines from the 'age of steam'in Brunel's B Shed, as photographed by
Hooper in the early 1900s. Boulton, C. Whatley, H. Blake, W. Bullock, J. Cook, G. Gosling, J. Lintern,
J. Knox, I. Brown, H. Hinder. These names are handwritten in this order on the back of the photograph.
(Paul Williams' Hooper Collection)

Railwaymen in the 'age of diesel'. 'Maintenance' was coveted work. Several maintenance gangs were
based in 33 Shop, c.1981/2. This is chargeman Terry Woodman's gang. From left to right, back: Norman
Taylor, Harry Newman, Dave Dillon, -?-, Terry Woodman. Front: John Harman, Dave Ross, Tony Pearce.
Other gang member Andy Binks is taking the photograph.

Employment at such an age was not uncommon, indeed it would have been the expectation. Children of even younger years had been employed in factories since the beginning of industrialisation, particularly in the textile mills. In most working-class families it would have been imperative for the children to be useful and/or 'earn their keep' as soon as was possible. On leaving school, whether at thirteen, fourteen or fifteen (the school leaving age was raised to fifteen in 1947), and as long as they had the necessary school 'leaving certificates', young boys would have to 'fill-in' time before they started their apprenticeships. (This changed in the 1960s when they left school at sixteen and went straight into 'training'.) The pre-apprentice period could be 'outside' as an errand boy but was usually inside the Works as an office boy in the foremen's offices, sometimes even in the main offices, or, more likely, working on the shop floor. Being an 'office boy' was one of 'the best times' of their lives and most who had been one talk about it fondly. It was a job that did not change much over time. An 'office boy' ran errands, although there were also regular, routine responsibilities attached like delivering mail, making the tea, or washing up the cups. The duties of Ernest Radway, an office boy in 19C Shop in the 1920s, included: 'dusting all the office desks, commencing with the foreman's, carefully ensuring that all the items, such as wire gauge, pliers, knives etc., were placed precisely in their correct positions.' Being an 'office boy' gave the lads immense freedom to roam, taking them all over the Works and even 'up town'. This feeling of 'freedom' appeared to permeate into their behaviour and circulars over the years often complain about their unrestrained conduct, such as that in November 1885 when Loco Works' Manager Carlton wrote to all foremen: 'Mr Hall of the Loco Offices reports that some of the foremen's office boys are in the habit of whistling, shouting or larking [yes, larking again!] in the corridor when they go up to the offices.' Mr Carlton threatens that: 'if found doing so after this notice they will be severely dealt with.' In February 1911 the office boys are yet again in the bad books. Circular No.2033 states: 'A good many of the office boys appear to be slovenly and ill-mannered. Please arrange for your clerk to train them in discipline and call your attention to any which it may be considered undesirable to retain in the service.' Years later they are indeed 'severely dealt with' by C.B. Collett, then CME, who, walking from the main Works entrance tunnel to his office, noticed office boys 'kicking a ball and generally fooling around'. He acted immediately and decisively as Ernest Radway remembers: 'An edict was issued that the number of office boys was to be reduced by 50%. In 19 Shop all the others boys except me were transferred to other work, but strangely enough it did not seem to increase my work load – nor my tips!' This element of 'tipping' was something to be relished by office boys as it greatly improved their take-home money. Radway remembers he was able to enhance his wages by changing the privilege ticket orders, obtained from the shop office, into tickets for the workmen; Swindon to Paddington at 4s 10d meant a 2d tip (change from 5s), Bristol Temple Meads was 2s 6½d , not so good at usually 1½d, but Trowbridge at 1s 9d was a real winner at 3d change, all probably increasing his income by 3–4s per week. At Christmas he was told to make a 'tip-tin' and stand by the checking-in station (i.e. the 'check-board'). Mr Mann, the foreman, started off the collection with a very generous 2s. In all Radway collected £2 12s 6d. Many years later Jim Starley also remembers the kindness of the men he ran errands for: 'Going round doing jobs you would be given little tips. At Christmas time they expected the office boys to go round everybody and say "Happy Christmas" with your special tip-tin. It was good. It would be about £11 or £12. First year I bought a snooker table and second year a pair of binoculars.' Other 'benefits' came from being an office boy and Tony Tucker remembers the 'lessons in life' he learned during his time in the main offices:

This photograph of the men of the Rail (Rolling) Mills was taken a few years before the First World War. It could have been taken by William Hooper, who was active with his camera in the Works at this time and was a neighbour of Albert Ernest Dawes (front row, fourth from right). It is a social document in its own right, showing the 'hierarchy' amongst the men with the workers in flat caps and their 'uniform' of waistcoats, neckerchiefs and, surprisingly considering the dirty work, white shirts, whilst the men in suits – the under-foremen in trilby and foremen in bowler hats – display their senior status and ranking. The fashion for moustaches is strongly favoured by the older men. The young lads in front could have been as young as eleven or twelve, while the old man sat in the middle of the front row could have been as old as seventy or eighty, as, in the days before 'pensions', it was not uncommon to work until you couldn't physically work anymore.

Albert Ernest Dawes was employed as a 'shingler' – one of the 'roller-men'. Albert had to wear metal plates on his legs for protection, yet even so his clothes were frequently burnt and he suffered at least one very nasty accident. Despite his dangerous labour Albert worked until he was seventy and had an active and manual 'outside' life looking after his large family of eight children – tending his long garden and allotment, getting water from the well (later by hand pump) doing all the family's shoe repairs, playing in Stratton Band and being Secretary to Upper Stratton Reform Club for forty-four years.

My birthday was on the 9 July which was during the Trip holiday, so I was 15 when I started work in 1951, immediately after the holiday. I started as office boy in 21 Accounts. My top Boss was H.W. Gardner who was chief accountant. He apparently insisted that he had a boy to do his running around for him [girls were also employed as 'office girls'] so I was the only office boy in the main offices. The only other boy was in the Drawing Office at the top of the building.

The job consisted of starting in the post room to sort out all the mail, which took about ¾ to 1 hour in time. Then I had to take the Time Book into every office to have everybody's work time entered. Next job was to wash up everybody's cup after break time, not sure how many but over a hundred a day, which was doubled when the office girl from 22 Accounts was out sick, which was frequent. It was a bit of a shock to me after going to a boy's school having to do the washing up with all the other office girls. Bit of an eye-opener that was.

Most of work for the office was carrying different kinds of forms to the other offices in the building and about the factory – as far down as the Con Yard one-way to as far as the station the other. I also had to go up town to do shopping for different people. A regular journey was to Boots, which was at the bottom of the town then, to get Mr Gardner's shaving stuff. I was office boy for about eighteen months.

For others, the majority, the less fortunate perhaps, it was into the shops. For many young lads this was something of a traumatic experience as Roy Taylor remembers:

I went in the factory in May 1938. I went in tapping nuts and screwing bolts in the scraggery. It was queer because I was told to come in clean clothes and then I got put into the scraggery where it was filthy. My overwhelming memory of in there was it smelt like anything. It was that 'white water' they used to work the machines, a mixture of water and rape oil. It was very repetitive work, you had to do hundreds a day. Had to do a binful which was weighed, that's how you got paid, by the weight.

Lots of repetitive monotonous work was kept for the boys, as Roy Blackford discovered doing his time in Saw Mill No.2 Shop:

We used to make all the flag poles for the guards. We had a machine called 'a rounder'. You put the square pieces of timber in and they'd come out at the other end, barrel like. Also the blinds sticks. When they had blinds, [on the carriage windows] they had round sticks at the bottom. Well they were cut out of ash and they were 3in square and you'd sit there with a bundle of these on this 'rounder' feeding them through and they would go through and then you gather them up and then you had a pencil sharpener-type thing which you just pushed them in and you finished up with a point on one end. Boys' jobs, monotonous, boring.

Whilst the umbrella term 'railwaymen' identified and addressed all those men who worked on the railways, Company, locality, workshop and type of work all played an important and influential role in railway culture and individual worker identity.[1] It was the apprenticeship that moulded the man-to-be and, once completed, stamped him in the image he would carry for the rest of his working life (as was the expectation when entering the railways right up until after the middle of the twentieth century), so, to quote Frank Saunders talking of his own and his father's time in the Works spanning the decades from the 1900 to 1960s, 'once a 'Loco Man' you were a 'Loco Man' for life'. The PRO holds a document which identifies the first railwaymen engaged at the Works in 1843, as cited in Alan Peck's book:

Foremen	6
Clerks (Time Office and Stores)	14
Enginemen	48
Firemen	50
Stationary Enginemen	3
Cleaners, Coke men, Labourers etc.	65
Fitters and Erectors	55
Turners	10
Contractors	60
Men at Machines	7
Carpenters and plumbers	6
Coppersmiths	2
Brass Foundryman	1
Blacksmiths	14
Springmakers	2
Strikers	14
Boilermakers and Wheelmakers	4
Painters	2
General Labourers	25
Boys	35

Norman Townsend, as pictured in *The Railway Gazette* of 12 May 1950 working on turning crown firebox stays, had trained as a machinist, which was classed as 'semi-skilled'. During the war he was put on lathes. Eventually, after he had worked about five years doing this 'skilled' work, he was 'upgraded' but he had to fight for it.

Dressed in their distinctive 'uniform' of flat cap, white shirt, waistcoat and moleskin trousers (which had greater resistance to burns), moulders go about their work. 'Jack' Fleetwood, a moulder, experienced the 'skill division': 'My father worked for 47 years "Inside". He was only semi-skilled so all they offered me was rough painter, machinist or moulding.' He picked moulding for me because it was 2s more on the rate. 'Jack' nevertheless was fiercely proud of his work.

Coach construction required 'first-class' skills. Coach frames were constructed of wood even in the 1960s, as Roy Blackford, a coach finisher, remembers:

A lot of it was still handcrafted in those days. When the 'body' came across from the Body Shop, it would be basically a shell and then we would go to work on it – everything you could see, the ceilings, the glass, the doors, the toilets, we would fix and finish the lot.

What defined a railwayman in general was the Company he worked for, what defined the man in the workshop was his level of skill. A craftsman wore his skill like a mantle. It was what defined him both as a railwayman and as a man. It gave him his identity both inside and outside the Works. It placed him within the pecking order of his community, his working community and his social community. 'Skill' was a valuable commodity; it cost to achieve it, either through payment of a 'premium' or through years of working as cheap labour through one's training, and its 'value' also equated to more money-in-the-pocket of those who possessed it, so that those who worked in the Tool Room, the 'top-skill-shop' got extra on their rate. The men, and the unions, were very possessive of their 'skills' and 'skilled status' and guarded them jealously. The GWR also kept strict control over who could become 'a skilled man' insisting that only skilled men's sons could follow them into skilled jobs. This enabled the GWR to control the allocation of men to the different trades and categories and accommodate the Company's requirements. Sons whose fathers were in unskilled positions had to tolerate this thoroughly unfair practice and accept the position the Company decided they could have. The skills levels on the railways in respect of industrial workers can be defined broadly in three categories: the tradesmen who undertook a long apprenticeship; the semi-skilled worker who did not undertake an apprenticeship but learnt his 'skills' training on the job like a fitter's mate; the 'unskilled' i.e. labouring grades who did work that required no prior knowledge or know-how and could be performed by anyone. John Atwell explains:

> Trades were classified 'first' or 'second' according to complexity, custom and practice and in negotiations with and between the different trade unions. Fitters, turners, coach finishers, boilermakers were first class; electricians, road wagon builders, plumbers and coppersmiths were all second class. First class trades received higher wage rates but the bigger difference was in social status.

Even amongst railwaymen themselves there was disagreement about what was a 'skilful job' and what was not, as Roy Blackford expressed: 'I mean the machinists, that was always a laugh really as they were all highly skilled at their job but they were always paid on a lower rate than we were.'

Pattern-makers were amongst the elite of tradesmen but moulders were only semi-skilled, the same as rough-painters and tractor drivers. Frank Hayward, a brass moulder, recalled the level of his status in relation to the reality of the skill level required, when he wrote to the *Evening Advertiser* in March 1986: 'The job was looked down upon as the lowest of the low, but it was a very skilled type of work as there were many kinds of metal requiring different treatments in the making of the moulds.' Roy Blackford, on the other hand, was a coach finisher, a first-class trade, in his words: 'A wonderful trade. During all the years I worked for the railway I worked on everything from horse boxes to royal saloons. It was wonderful work.'

This 'categorisation' of skills created many areas of tension within the Works that were exploited by both the GWR in its time, the crafts guilds, and, later, the unions, especially during the war periods when the men guarded their skills even more jealously against male and female dilutees, and they were still guarding them after Nationalisation, in fact, right up until the time when the Works was in so much jeopardy of closing that the men had to become more 'flexible' in the way they husbanded these skills. Most men, like Bill Bryant and his father before him, were fully aware of the hierarchical impositions based on skill that kept workers knowing their place and *in* their place. In his memoir *Nobody had Reverence* Bryant wrote:

> Although my father was proud of his job he knew full well that his position in the gradings in the factory was of a low key … A system of inequality was bred into the workforce of the town. They were divided by craft, they were divided by wage rates and they were divided by opportunities.[2]

Your area of skill gave you your working identity. Traditionally railwaymen expected to carry their identity – e.g. 'engineer' 'fitter turner erector' 'carriage body maker' 'moulder' 'wheelwright' 'carpenter' – with them through their whole working lives. When so much work was 'hand-done' things changed hardly at all as Peter Withers, a sheet metal worker, found: 'I used to make all sorts – guards for machines, tea urns, oil rings for the oil pads for the steam locos, steam engine number plates. Then the front of the diesels were done not by presses, all by hand. So the tools of trade hardly changed over the years as it was so much hand work.' With the changes from steam to diesel, from wood to metal, from 'railway' to more general engineering, however, many men in the Works found their brand of skills diminished or disposed of and their seniority of service lost its status in the jostle to be part of the new technological world *and* remain in employment, as Jim Rogers experienced: 'In the 1970s my trade almost died out. I got sent down the Con Yard burning up old wagons for scrap. After a year of that I got drafted on to a boilermaking job, then I had four years in the Saw-Mill, then back on the boilermaking activity until the Works closed.' Mike White also experienced this need to change skills: 'I trained as a fitter-turner-erector (1956-1961) and had to retrain as a welder in 1978 and do 'wagon-bashing for a time, then a period on the lathes in the Machine Shop, then on to diesel repairs in the BD Shop.'

'Dieselisation' brought a new dilemma to the skills debate as Roger Hayes who started up the new workshop for the repair of diesel engines recalls:

> Anybody who did any manufacturing activity in the Works was a tradesman. They were all time-served, skilled men, so there were a lot of common core skills, but it was the knowledge of how diesel engines worked that they lacked. We were given mostly young people who had just come out of their apprenticeship and some who had returned from war, but a lot of sub-components, which were repetitive procedures, were done by the older workmen or those who had been disabled. Because we made everything in the Works, there was always something that could be done by the workmen.

Later, in the dying days of the railway workshop industry, 're-skilling' i.e. changing skills, or adapting your skill to a different craft, or being prepared to be 'flexible' within your trade identity, became the only way to remain a railwayman still in work, as the tradesmen in the Works found in the difficult 1960s, '70s and '80s.

During the Steam era the work required to build locomotives, and later wagons and carriages, spawned hundreds of different jobs in all trades, many with evocative-sounding names that no longer exist today. Many of these names resonate with their era and with the nature of the work done, as in early days the 'names' given to the different workers simply reflected the nature of

Left: Carriage-side jobs were held to be cleaner, more 'gentlemanly' and 'creative'. Many of the sign-painters, like this man painting the simplified GWR roundel introduced in 1934, were also skilled artists who exhibited regularly in the GWR annual Arts & Crafts Exhibitions, men like Reginald 'Ewart' Bezer, who did a six-year apprenticeship between 1908–1914 and went on to work 'Inside' for forty-seven years, twenty-five as a chargeman. One of his best memories was being recalled after his retirement and overseeing the repainting of the *City of Truro* on which he did the intricate crest and scroll.

Below: Fitting Shop, Carriage & Wagon Dept in the early 1900s. Jim Osman holds that C & W fitters, who were always known as '5/8th fitters' by those on the Loco side, were much maligned and put down. 'We had very little to do with carriages, much more to do with maintenance,' he says.

the work they did, especially in the 'hot-shops'. Names such as fire-lighter, fire-watcher, the rollers & roughers, the knocker-out, the drag-out man, the die sinkers, ladle runners, stay-tappers and pull-up boys, all paint vivid pictures almost to the point of seeing the named man working before your eyes. In 1943 a list was made of the different grades who had volunteered for the Home Guard. Its fascination is that it reads like an ABC of the working lives of the railwaymen then in the Works:

Analysts, Angle Iron Smiths, Apprentices, Armature Winder, Axlebox Trimmer, Axle Turner,

Batteryman, Blacksmith, Blacksmith's Asst., Boiler Attendant, Boilersmith, Boilersmith's Asst., Boilerwasher, Boilerscruffer, Brakebox Fitter, Bolt Maker, Bolt Repairer, Brass Finisher, Brickarchman, Bricklayer, Bricklayer's Asst., Boiler Attendant, Buffer, Brake and Drawgearman,

Callman, Case Hardener, Carpenter, Checkers, Piecework etc. Carriage Repairers, Carriage Cleaners, Carriage Fitters, Carriage Fitter's Asst., Carriage Lifter, Clerk, Coach Bodymaker, Coach Finisher, Coach Trimmer, Coalman, Coppersimth, Coppersmith's Asst., Crane-man and Crane-Driver, Coremaker,

Draughtsman, Driver,

Engine Cleaner, Electrical Fitter, Electrician, Electrician A.T.C., Erector, Examiners, Elec., Examiners Carr & Wagon,

Firedroppers and Fire Cleaners, Furnaceman, Furnaceman's Asst., Firelighter, Firewatcher, Floorlayer, Fireman, Fitter, Fitter's Asst., Forgeman, Forgeman's Asst.,

Gas Fitter, Gas Fitter's Asst., Gas Makers, Gland Packers, Grease Maker & Oil Blender, Greaser, Gaugeman,

Hydraulic Engineman, Hydraulic Repairer, Hydraulics Labourer, Hydraulic Fireman, Holder-up, Hammer Boy,

Inspector - Shop, Inspector - Boiler, Inspector – Material,

Labourer, Lead Burner, Lamp Attendant, Lifter, Lifter's Asst.,

Machinist, Machinist Boy, Machinary Attendant, Main Layer, Millwright, Messenger, Moulder,

Painter, Patternmaker, Pipe Fitter, Pipe Layer, Plater, Plater's Asst., Photographer, Pumpman, Plumber, Puncher & Shearsman, Polisher, Porter – Office, Packing Splicer, Platelayer,

Rivetters, Rivet Hotters, Riggers,

Saddlers, Stripper & Cleaner, Scaffolder, Steam Hammerman, Saw Doctor, Sawyer,

Sawyer's Asst., Shedman, Spotter (Roof), Shunter, Sheet Metal Worker, Stationary Engineman, Steam Raiser, Storesman, Switchboard Attendant, Striker, Sub-Station Attendant, Shift-Engineer,

Timber Marker, Timekeeper, Tinsmith, Toolman, Tube Cleaner, Tuber, Turner,

Vacuum Brake Examiner,

Wagon Writer, Wagon Builder, Wagon Repairer, Wagon Repairer's Asst., Wagon Rivetter, Water Pumping Engineman, Water Fitter, Watchman, Wheelwright, Welder, Weighman, Wireman, Window Attendant, Wheel Turner, Wood Machinist, Wood Machinist Boy, Wire Ropeman.

These are not the whole by any means. Many will have already dropped by the wayside, and, come the era of diesel, many of those cited would disappear too.

Whilst 'railwaymen' may appear united as a body, the divisions between themselves were profound and real. In Swindon Works such divisions were numerous. The main one was 'Loco' versus 'Carriage & Wagon', which can be visualised as the 'aggressive engineer' against the 'gentlemanly carpenter', the first doing work that got your hands dirty and the latter work where one needed one's hands to be clean. It was the 'greasy overall' versus the 'clean white apron', both symbols of status and both worn with pride; indeed, before the First World War, coach fitters, a 'top-notch trade' made a point of cycling home at dinner time wearing their white aprons to 'show off' their status to the world at large. Each side, of course, thought theirs was the best.

Alan Lambourn's father, Reginald, a blacksmith, experienced this 'divide' or, as Alan puts it 'the strong identity difference', when, after being trained and employed Loco side, he was 'laid off from F Shop in the early 1920s and then taken back on some time later but into 14 Shop (C & W side). It took a long time before my father was accepted being a former 'Loco-man' but having proved that he was not only capable but also willing to adapt to the C & W policy of doing things, he was accepted and given his 'C & W' credentials!' Ironically, forty years later, Alan found himself in the same position. Returning to the Works in 1965 after a spell of some years away, he was offered a position as 'turner' in 15 Shop. He recalls: 'I accepted the offer rather reluctantly and with serious reservations as, being a Loco-man, to enter C & W territory was literally like going abroad!' Percy Warwick also remembers that: 'At one time there was always that little bit of animosity between Loco and Carriage side, although we were all in the Works, it sometimes felt like it was two separate factories. If Loco side had a dispute, they would come across and try to get Carriage side to support them, but they didn't always get it.' This rivalry persisted even after the C & W had moved over to the Loco side, even into the 1970s, as Bob Gale found:

> While in 21 office I became aware of the divide between Loco and Carriage side men, mostly remarks were made in jest but sometimes not. I'm afraid in later years I was guilty as well when I had to associate myself with Carriage side methods of working. None of this though ever got out of hand, as I said, it was mostly leg pulling.

There were many other divisions that created tensions such as skilled versus semi-skilled or unskilled; shop floor versus office; union versus union; union versus management; workers versus bosses; during the General Strike of 1926 it was striker versus non-striker or 'scabs'; and of course railwaymen versus railwaywomen! Always there was a 'them' and 'us'. Alfred Williams says of the early 1900s workmen structures:

> The chiefs of departments are usually more or less rivals … The same … maybe said of the foremen of several divisions, while the workmen were about indifferent in this respect … Transfers from one shop to another are seldom made and never from department to department. One would think that the various divisions of the works were owned by separate firms, or people of different nationalities, such formidable barriers appear to exist between them …

Decades later in the 1930s whilst working in the AV Shop, Hugh Freebury discovered these barriers in practical terms. He writes how at the end of his first day as a rivet-hotter he went to wash his hands in the nearest water trough. 'Oh, no you don't,' shouted one of the fitters aggressively, elbowing me out of the way. 'Go and wash yer 'ands in the bucket.' He was referring to the large tin of water kept at the side of the forge for regularly cooling the tongs. 'I thought they wouldn't let you get away with it,' remarked Fred Turney, who had already washed in the bucket. 'They're a funny lot most fitters.' Later Hugh's father explained that 'the trough' was a jealously guarded 'privilege' that dated back some years previously to when the boilermakers had gone on strike demanding more pay than the fitters, wanting 47s for a basic week as against the fitters' 46s. The increase was granted and the fitters appeased with the offer of washing troughs and roller towels. Woe betide any boilermaker or boilermaker apprentice who thought he could use it! As Williams highlighted, this 'division' was exaggerated by most workmen being contained within their shed or workshop. It was always strictly against the rules to go wandering around from one shop to another, let alone between Loco to C & W sides. Williams writes about this:

> For them, all beyond their own sheds, except for a few personal friends and relatives, are total strangers. Though they may have been employed at the Works for half a century, they have never gone beyond the boundary of their own department ... for trespassing is strictly forbidden and sharply punished where detected. Thus the workman's sphere is very narrow and limited.

A major factor, if not *the* major one, behind the 'division' between the men themselves (apart from whether they were 'Loco' or 'C & W') was that it made a significant difference to their take-home pay. The 'take-home pay' was based on a number of 'rates' – piecework rate; new work rate; 'specials' rate; flat rate; night work rate; war rate; all of which had to be factored into other considerations such as basic pay, overtime, bonus (or balance), 'dirty work enhancements' to name but some. The men worked in gangs. 'The gang' was part and parcel of the workshop culture. Unlike the pop song or playground chant: 'd'ja wanna be in my gang?' whose gang you ended up in, or stayed in, depended on 'those in charge' i.e. the foreman and/or the chargeman. 'The gang', whatever its size, became your 'working family' and its welfare affected your welfare! Harry Bruton worked on Loco side. During the Second Worls War he kept a very small day-to-day diary. He recorded only the major things that impacted on his life – the war; the weather; his family; the work; his gang:

1940

January

5 big boxes 10 x 6

8 Rationing began for ham eggs butter sugar. 10 x 6 boxes at work. Did a job for Mr
  Workman

17 Fitter in the morning marking off on Ambulance coaches

18 marked off on Ambulance coaches

19 rush on 10 x 6 boxes

F1 Blacksmith Shop Loco Works, 1956. The 'gang' are, from left to right: Len Tuck; Harold Akers, blacksmith (back to camera); Jim New, striker; Bill Smith, hammer driver, forging a piece under the hammer.

9 Shop Rail Car section 'gang' members. From left to right: John Charlesworth, Phil Corbyn, Mick Kocoz, and 'Bones' Bowden. John 'put in his time' from 1961–1986, when the Works closed. 'I managed to get my twenty-five-year Award for Long Service, I had a little brass carriage clock.'

Feb

1 N Keel back at work F Peaple out

5 Worked overtime on ambulance train. Harry Brine out and N Keel & apprentice out.
   Gang in mess

6 again work overtime. Dawkins on the gang, job going well

8 Harry Brine died, he was at work last Friday

9 F Bowker died. Finished 3 ambulance coaches

14 Bill Henry not so well

15 Bill Henry out again. Tested Westinghouse brake on 3 ambulance coaches

19 Fred Austin made Foreman in Mr Burchell's place

20 Coal shortage 2 cwt for week. Went to Labour meeting

24 Sat – Clock put forward

March

1 fed up with work. 10 rail and timbers bogies to be done, lot of work on gang

4 Bert Day back at work. E Lopes on the gang. No balance

5 Worked overtime busy on rail and timber bogies. All the gang in

10 Meat ration tomorrow

30 Sat – Harry married at Christchurch about 70 there

April

1 still on overtime fed up with it.

3 More planes brought down over North Sea – 52 since beginning of war

18 Mr Robins spoke to me about things. Still on overtime.

22 did not work overtime

24 G at work, had rotten cold

Harry's short, terse entries highlight the importance and the impact of the gang's well-being on each individual member (as well as highlighting the hard, dreary effects of the war). In terms of who got the best jobs for the best rates it was literally one gang against another. Which gang you were in and who was in your gang and how your gang worked affected your pocket as Hugh Freebury vividly remembers in respect of his father's pay: 'the balance earned by the Planers' gang of my father, was the worst paid in the AM Shop, which was lucky to get 10% or even 5% and was often 'in debt.'

During the Second World War the thought that the war recruited women would adversely affect the earnings of the gang was one of the reasons for the men's initial reluctance to work with them. Happily this proved not to be the case. Mrs E P. recalls when she worked as a rivet-hotter: 'I was on a good gang and got good money – sometimes I got more than my Dad, he wasn't on a good gang. Mind you I worked hard, 'cos I was saving up for my little home … we all were, all us girls. The men were pleased with us, there was no slacking.' Tony Tucker remembers how well the women worked in 1951:

There were three men on the tapping gang, Dave Sims (chargeman), Bert Hedges (underchargeman) and a man called John. There were women working there too. I can

Above: During the Second World War women had to become 'gang' members despite men's initial resistance because of worries regarding their 'take-home' pay. Shortly after the war women were actively recruited into some of the workshops through male family members working in there, such as hammer-drivers Pam and Peggy Pinnegar. 'Inside' were their father, Albert John 'Jackie' (holder-upper V Boiler Shop), brothers Gordon (boilermaker V Boiler Shop), Derick (machinist AE Shop) and Ken (blacksmith welder F2 Shop), who encouraged the girls with promises of 'a man's wage'.

Hammer-drivers F1 and F2 Blacksmith Shops Loco works, c.1950. From left to right, back row: Lorna Lawrence, Emmie Thompson, Harry ? (Blacksmith), Margaret Stone, Wally Waite (Blacksmith), Minnie Hacker, Pam Pinnegar. Front row: -?-(Labourer), Peggie Pinnegar, Vi Smith, Peggy Pedrick, Betty ? Phil ?

Left: Teamwork does it every time. Pete Kelly, chargeman and Ian Heslop pouring 1,120lb of molten brass from a ½ ton Induction Furnace into a LG4 ladle with a capacity of 280lb. (1983)

remember one was called Blondie. There was a lady on the automatic tapping machine which was always going wrong. I started on a tapping machine, which had six drivers running all the time. I worked with a lady named Elsie. I found her friendly. We worked three taps each. You had to put the tap in the driver while it was running, enter it into a blank nut and let it cut a thread in the nut. When there was about 4 or 5 nuts on the shank of the tap you had to remove the tap (still running) and throw the nuts in a bin. It cut your hands to pieces. Where you kept picking up the nuts from the tray it looked as is you had been biting your nails where they had been worn away. We had to do a bin full a day. I don't know how she did it but Elsie always did more than anyone else and that's after taking a couple of long toilet breaks [the women had a long way to walk to their toilets]. I can't remember any problems with the women being there. As long as they earned their money I presume everything was fine.

Peter Withers, a sheet metal worker, remembers that: 'When the all-steel coach came along, gangs would battle for what they would do. My gang made all the panels.' Which gang you were in also affected your 'standing'. Andy Binks had the good fortune to 'come out of his time' in 1974 and, because of certain unusual circumstances, go straight into 'the Maintenance gang' in the Hooter House. This was normally unheard of. 'Maintenance' went to long-time servers. It was a gang of 'senior' status. Other men, waiting for that 'step up', and the unions were very unhappy about it and tried to get him moved out, but his chargeman, Roy Sessford, was determined to hang on to him and he was more than happy to stay.

Another reason for the 'each gang for itself' mentality was that for a great deal of the life of the Works' men lived in constant anxiety over the security of their jobs. Whilst some experienced 'a-job-for-life, like Mike White's maternal grandfather, Richard Eldridge Richards, who spent his whole working life, from fourteen until seventy-two years old, on the tenders in D Shed, for many others 'shortening-hands', 'lay-offs', 'redundancies', as well as many episodes of short-time working, were a grim reality, sometimes not just once, but often several times. Percy Warwick tells how:

Quite often men would be in and out. Some would go to Oxford to the motor industry and then when it was o.k. for the Company, they would be called back. This seemed to happen quite regularly, perhaps when it was time to report to the Shareholders! It seemed to be mostly from the Carriage side. Our neighbour, Mr Long, he went to Oxford to the cars a few times, and then got called back.

These 'divisions' in the Works came with a lot of historical baggage. Back in its infancy work divisions came about not through 'labour' identity, as a 'turner' would be expected to 'turn' anything needed on any part of the job that was being done, but rather through divisions of 'gangs', i.e. which 'contractor' or 'foreman' you worked for. The structure of hierarchy taken into the workshops was a system already established in the building of the canals and then subsequently the railway track, when work was sold by the Company to individual men, i.e. 'contractors' who then sold it on to the 'sub-contractor' (or head of 'the gang') who would bid for 'parts' of the job the contractor had. Each sub-contractor had his own 'gang' made up of different tradesmen and labourers whom he had 'hired' and therefore could also 'fire'. Each 'job' price would be separately negotiated for and it was up to the 'chargeman' as

Roger Hayes, left, measuring a connecting rod bearing and John Smith, right, examining the piston, which has just been removed from the very first Maybach 1100bhp 12-cylinder engine reconditioned in the Works, 1961. Roger started 'Inside' in 1957 aged twenty-two, qualified in machining and repair of internal combustion engines. He hit an opportune moment for the changeover to diesels. Together with Geoff Webber he started up the diesel engine shop, called 'BD' Shop. With his much-needed 'new' skills, Roger was destined to be a fast-track man and within the year he had been madeup to chargeman: 'I co-ordinated the work activity, dished out the work, booked in their bonuses, sorted the spares, all that sort of thing. I was also the communicator between the foreman and other groups.' Roger went on up the ladder to follow in both his grandfathers' footsteps and become a foreman.

they became known (presumably called such because he was 'in charge' of the gang of men and/or negotiated the 'charge' for the job) to get the best price and deal he could. In the early times of the Works there is some confusion between the terms 'contractors' and 'foremen' and the early role of what is later identified as 'chargeman', but what is established is the power base of those who become known as 'the foremen' and 'the chargeman' terms which are then continued right until the end of the Works. These early arrangements were accepted by the Company and were later operated on both the Loco-side and the Carriage & Wagon side, and were then broadened and reinforced by the craft-based structures of the workforce and the hierarchical operating systems within GWR's own management, presumably on the basis of 'divide and rule', but they were also later kept in strict operation by the Unions to meet their purposes, especially after Nationalisation. These structures remained basically unchanged throughout the time of the Works. John Attwell recalls how these systems worked in the 1940s:

The A Shop (A1 and A2 Shop combined) became the largest covered workshop in Europe in the 1920s, covering some 11 acres. It was particularly notable for its long 'road' or 'traverser', about 520ft, that went in, through and out of the shop, and also its sixty pits and its four massive 100-ton electric cranes which could lift the whole loco off its wheels. Here the magnificent *King George V* is stripped down for refurbishment in 1983 prior to preservation. Below, the crane lifts Western-class D1023 in the diesel era.

The shop was run by a foreman, who had … piece work checkers [Inspectors] under him responsible for checking the quality. Workers were organised into about half a dozen gangs, each with a chargeman who was responsible for doing the books. Each job had a price and each gang would undertake part of a job. If there was a dispute over which trade was responsible for a job the unions would sort it out but this was rare.

'Chargeman' was an idiosyncratic job, but one that was the same during steam and through dieselisation. It was the job that took the craftsman from purely 'production' into the realms of 'management'. The chargemen played several important roles but most importantly 1) they sorted the money (or 'worked' the money as some said) particularly 'the balance' (bonus) and 2) they were the buffer between foreman and men. Booking the bonus or 'working' the money so that men never felt a loss in their pockets, was a tricky job; working it so that the piecework rate always worked out to be acceptable to both men and management, and, as 'balance' was originally paid alternate weeks, working it so that more balance arrived at helpful times, e.g. just before Trip or Christmas, is what made some chargemen more popular than others. Ernest Fischer remembers how it worked when he started in 1946:

> When I started I was on £5.10, and then £6.10.00 on the balance every other week — then later they shifted it to the balance every week. We were on piece work rates, half-a-crown for steam pipe, 9d for drilling out a broken stud and putting a new stud in, things like that. The chargehand would book it all in. It went into the shop and we all shared it. About forty fitters and I don't know how many labourers.

'The balance' could be paid out either for a gang or for a shop as Bob Townsend explains:

> A 'gang balance' was where one gang shared out the 'balance'. If, say, there were ten gangs all on individual gang balances, this could lead to a little bit of feeling about others earning more. In a 'Shop balance' all balances went into a pool and everybody got the average. This was a fairer system. I think in the BD Shop we had a 'Shop balance.

Pat Sullivan recalls the 'strangeness' of his balance experience: 'It was funny really because it seemed no matter how hard you worked, the fitter's bonus seemed to be about the same. Sometimes you used to get a little bit more but they used to say the chargeman kept a little bit back this week for when you've got a low week.' If you had a good chargeman, one who was in with the foreman, this could make a lot of difference to your 'balance' as Hugh Freebury found: 'The balance varied from gang to gang, but since my chargehand was a particular favourite of the foreman, who was supposed to decide the price for all the various jobs, with a Piecework Inspector to check these, our gang usually did well with an average of 50% balance every other week.' The chargeman was influential in other ways too – he could decide your fate as Percy Warwick remembers: 'In the old days it wasn't necessarily last on first off. It was a case of if your face fitted you stayed, if it didn't you went. It was really up to how the chargeman felt about you. He could influence things. My old father was lucky 'cos he never had the sack, he was never laid off. Same as meself.'

Right: Gilbert Victor Norman 'Joe' Taylor in his chargeman's box, a symbol of authority. 'Joe' went in as boilermaker apprentice in 1911. He was a plater in the AV Shop and worked on the footplates and the frames, but not on the boilers. His son Roy remembers: 'He stayed all his working life in the Works, retiring at sixty-five, and he didn't get anything. I can't remember him ever being laid off though. That's quite something for them days.'

Below: Diesels brought new names to the shops. The first diesel 'shop' started in the B Shed was known as BD Shop (i.e. B Shed Diesel Shop). It rapidly outgrew this workspace and had to be moved to a much larger one. The old Iron Foundry was refurbished for this purpose and became 9 Shop as seen here. 9 Shop was a huge dmu production line. Starting at the far end of the photograph and working forwards the engine underwent several processes – dismantling, cleaning, examination and assembly – prior to being dispatched for testing.

Working in 'shops'

If you had asked a Works tradesman where he worked he would have answered 'Inside'. Asked again 'where?' and he'd say 'R Shop' or 'O Shop', or even '15 Shop' or '14 Shop'. For railwaymen and their families 'shops had a double meaning', as Stuart Butler wrote in his poem *Shopping in the Railway Works*, for the Works comprised a number of different workshops, spoken of just as 'shops'. Later, after the Works closure, these same 'shops' were converted for commercial use into a 'new shopping experience'. For Stuart it was a strange experience to go 'shopping' in the workshops 'where my dad used to work'. In the beginning it was easy – just A, B, C. A Shed – the first 'engine establishment'. B Shed – for repairing the magnificent broad-gauge locomotives. C Shed – with its hydraulic overhead crane made by Napier in 1844. Then it started to get more complicated as 'sheds' were modified, becoming 'shops', and more 'shops' were added. Later numbers were used for shops on the new Carriage Works and Wagon Works. Company circulars flew thick and fast informing what the changes in 'names' or 'letters' were. Originally letters and numbers identified the buildings, not the type of work done in them, but when all the departments came into the one area in the late 1960s all 'work activities' were then identified by numbers for costing purposes, no matter where the work was carried out, although the men still spoke of the shops by their original titles.

Stuart Butler writes in his poem of the magic and mystery of 'an alphabet of shops' in the early 1960s:

A Shop, A Erecting Shop, A Shop Engine Testing Plant and A Shop Extension;
B Shop, Boiler AV Shop, Boiler House and Brass Turning and Fitting Shop,
C Shop, Carpenter's Shop, Carriage Finishers (No.7) Shop,
Carriage Repair (No.19) Shop, Carriage and Wagon Construction (No.24) Shop, Carriage
    and Wagon (No.16) Shop, Concentration Yard, Coppersmith's Shop and Cylinder Shop,
Diesel Engine Repair Shop, DMU lifting Shop and Drop Hammer Shop,
Engine Repair Shop and Erecting Shop [Electrical Shop]
Forge and Smith's Shop,
Grinding Shop and Iron Foundry,
Lifting Shop, Locomotive Paint Shop,
Locomotive Wheel (AV) Shop,
New Points and Crossing Shop and Points and Crossing (X) Shop
Road Motor (No.17) Shop and Rolling Mill,
Steam Hammer Shop and Stamping Shop,
Tender Shop, Trimming Shop, Truck Shop and Turning Shops,
Wagon Frame (No.13) Shop, Wheel Shop and Wheelsmith's Shop.

The nature of the work done in the 'shop' informed the nature of the man that did it – Gordon Ing holds that: 'the men in the Stamping Shop were some of the hardest men in the whole country' – and the nature of the man can be judged by one of the Works' slogans – 'if its difficult consider it done, the impossible may take a little longer'. The benchmark of 'impossible' for the men of Swindon Works was set back in 1846 when the GWR decided to completely build its own engines. The Works had been established merely to repair and sometimes rejig and

Many shops ran their own clubs and teams. Meet the 'Iron Foundry J Shop Football Team 1930'. Seated first left is Albert Dawes and second left is best mate Harold Titcombe, always known as 'Ticker'. Albert gave up football once he had a family as, he said, he 'couldn't afford to be off work with an injury'. Unfortunately he had to have several weeks off when he was seriously burnt as a result of a work accident.

improve the rolling stock bought in by the Company from other sources. In reality this was a costly practice and they had started to part-build engines for freight work in 1845 but by 1846 the Company badly needed their own engine to haul passenger trains that would outstrip their rivals. The Board ordered Gooch to build 'a colossal locomotive working with all speed'. Alan Peck wryly comments: 'It is not quite clear whether this meant a fast locomotive or that they wanted it in a hurry! Perhaps they meant both, and they certainly got it.' The production of Gooch's locomotive, aptly named *The Great Western*, the first locomotive to be entirely built at Swindon, is part of the 'heroic' story of the Works. By continually working both day and night shifts, the men turned out the engine in just *thirteen weeks* – an incredible achievement when one remembers that it was still a time of man and muscle rather than man and machine. Constructing an engine 'in-house' started a trend that would influence the philosophy of the GWR and shape Company policy in the future, i.e. that whenever possible the GWR would always produce its own goods, from engines, carriages, wagons, its own tools, component parts, furniture, even down to its own recycled soap. This policy, along with the centralisation of

Railwaymen not only worked together, they played together too. Shop outings were a regular feature.
From left to right, back: Eric Walker, Jack Wheeler, Ernie Collins, Arthur Hatter, -?-, -?-, -?-. Front: Peter
Pragnell, Sam Jones of D Shop (Factory Maintenance).

'Up on the roof.' Front: -?-.
Centre: Frank Drew. Back:
Ken Baylis. Whenever
they could, railwaymen, of
whatever era, would resort to
'larking' around.

many working activities at Swindon, not only helped prolong the life of the Works, but also informed the thinking and attitudes of its workmen.

It is said that the different tradesmen displayed individual traits or natures such as Freebury found with fitters, and as Alfred Williams found with the boilermakers: 'the boiler makers are a bold and hardy class, sturdy in their views and outlook and very independent.' Such was the 'boldness' and sturdiness of their views that in 1912/1913 it led to protests of 'victimisation' against their members. In early 1913 'discharges' were made amongst the boilermen in V Shop, but to many they had more the feel of 'dismissals', as they appeared to be for political alliances and trade union activity. A new 'Rating System' had been introduced in December 1912, with the promise that there would be 'no cutting of the men's prices'. This system, along with a clock system that was allegedly 'for the purpose of costing the machines', was purported to be beneficial for men as well as the Company. The boilermen and their union, however, were against it as there appeared to be 'some significant alteration in the prices for boiler work', but the GWR's version was that 'the price rates have always been in a state of flux'. The union had been pushing for more men to join up and stand against a system where they could end up earning even less than 'the pound or a guinea a week as at present'. Just one month into the New Year the GWR were discharging around 200 men in the Boiler Shop, this at a time when Churchward was telling the Swindon Chamber of Commerce that: 'the factory which employs about 14,000 men was at the present moment turning out as much work as it had ever done.' The explanation given was that the men discharged had been working on short-time since November and the Company no longer wished 'to proceed further along these lines'. By February the number had risen to some 300. It was said this was due to overstocking of boilers and, therefore, a reduced need for men, yet many of these men were immediately replaced on their machines by others newly appointed. *The Daily Chronicle* asked: 'Are Liberal Workmen Penalised?' It reported that 'certain Foremen went through the shops enquiring 'Is he a Radical? Does he talk politics in the Shop?' The Company refuted such charges, even issuing a notice stating: 'the men were allowed to exercise their rights to belong to any political party without interference' although this was somewhat disingenuous as the GWR, like many, if not most, of the other railway companies, had from its early times, a history of being very anti-collective-representation. The GWR stated that their 'guiding principles' for selecting men was in order of three criteria: 1) men with recorded incidents against them; 2) single men with no responsibilities; 3) married men and long service men as a last resort. Despite this there appeared to be a great number of men with exemplary records, long service and large family responsibilities chosen for dismissal. The *Daily Chronicle* identifies a number of such cases:

C.E. Smith. 39 years 25 years in the service of the Company.
An excellent timekeeper who has not lost a single quarter of a day per year.
That Smith is an efficient workman is proved by his frequent selection for New Work during the last 11 years. No complaint has ever been made against him. As showing the respect in which he is held by his fellow workman … he completed his term of president of the Boilermakers No 1 Society, Swindon. He was elected by his fellow workmen second on the poll as their representative on the Court of Referees under the National Insurance Act Part 2. Smith has bought his home in Swindon. Another man put in his place.

F.J. Dyer, a driller. 12 years service. Married with five children. A thoroughly
efficient man against whom no complaint have ever been lodged … another man
put in his place.

Francis J. Lewis, boilermaker's helper, aged 34. Twenty and a half years service.
Married with five children. Has not lost a single quarter of a day in all his time of service. Has
only been absent from sickness once and that was five years ago. In his gang of thirty, many
younger men kept on.

This experience obviously stung and left a bad feeling with the workmen for later that year,
when the Canadian Pacific Railway began recruiting in Swindon, the *Daily Chronicle* reported
on 7 June: '300 leaving Swindon This Month … for Canada. The emigration of railwaymen
from Swindon this year sets up a record.'[3] The doggedness and hardiness of the boilermen can
be seen in Alfred Williams' comments written shortly after that time:

F1 Blacksmith Shop Loco Works 1956, or the 'Leica Studios' as designated on the walls of blacksmith
Eric Bradley's fire. Like William Hooper, Eric, left, was a keen photographer and took a series of
atmospheric photographs of 'his fire' and workmates during 1956, although obviously not this one.

This little photograph (taken by Andy Binks) of the tiny chargeman's box with chair and hanging jacket, the Noticeboard with umpteen official and unofficial notices, the Memorial to fallen comrades, the old work bench festooned with plants in old pots and kettles, the engineer's vice and the silly notice – DANGER – MEN WORKING ON PLANTS – sums up so much that is part and parcel of the Works' workshop men!

A short time ago a party of boilermen, who had been discharged from the town made weekly visits to the villages around pretending they had walked from Sunderland and Newcastle where a big strike had been declared … they called themselves a deputation empowered to collect money for their mates back home. Very soon trade in the railway town revived; the majority of the men were re-instated.

Whatever their trade or occupation, one thing shared by all workshop men was a keen sense of humour, mischievousness even, especially for practical jokes. Their humour often had an 'edge' of toughness, for which everyone, no matter low or high, male or female, was 'fair game'. Gordon Dickinson remembers this feeling in his first encounter with 'real' railwaymen, when, having just completed his first year in the WTS, he was taken on a 'visit' to see the Works:

We were then taken to where we would be working to meet our new 'mates' – this was the point I realised that I had chosen the right trade. These men were in contrast to most of the others clean and fairly tidy, a lot of them (the finishing gang) were wearing collar and ties, not too much sweat was in evidence and it all seemed quite civilised. These people were known as 'the silver arsed gang' … that was what I decided I was going to become. There was something in the way they looked at us, with an almost devilish wryness, that made me feel slightly wary of what was in store for us … as we stood there, dressed in our sparkling clean green (very apt) overalls the expression 'fresh meat' entered my head.

'Fresh meat' indeed, for there were no victims more open for leg-pulling and mickey-taking than the newly arrived apprentices, and they got the lot! Mrs Francis Wakely, who worked as an office girl in the Loco Stores, remembers these 'initiations' well: 'It happened all the time, lads being sent with chits for all sorts of daft things, rubber hammers, rubber rivets, a bucket of steam. One time it got so bad, probably after a new intake, that one of the supervisors got really mad. This lad had been sent for 'a shovel with holes in' so the supervisor ordered up the shovel and had it drilled with holes, then charged it to the gang. They were furious, but he said, "that was [what] the chitty said, so that's what you got" and they had to pay!' The most commonly talked of 'prank' by railwaymen was 'the stand and long weight'. Sent to the Stores or another

Whatever their job, shop, or office, Swindon Works railway men developed an early passion for music and music making together, whether singing, playing in bands of all kinds or orchestras. They would grab every moment to practice as here, the Staff Association Orchestra caught rehearsing in the dinner break.

part of the shop for a 'stand and long weight about five to ten' the lad would then be told to 'just stand over there for a mo while I deal with this will you' and after waiting patiently for some time, he would remind the man he was still there. 'Oh, how long have you been standing and waiting?' 'About five to ten minutes.' 'I think you've waited long enough then, don't you?' Penny drops. Laughs all round. The apprentices soon learned to join in the laughter and laugh at themselves. They had to, to survive. It was a 'rite of passage' that took them from boyhood to manhood. They learned to 'tough-it-out' and eventually 'get-one-over' on some other poor unsuspecting bloke! Other 'fresh meat' were the women war recruits. The jokes played on them often seemed to involve mice, rats and the dark! Jack Fleetwood remembers one such joke the men in the Foundry loved to play on the women core-makers in the Core-Shop. Once made, the women had to take their cores into the large brick stove and stack them for drying. Jack recalls, 'whilst they were inside one of the lads would slide the door shut. There was no light in the stove and it would have been really dark, then you'd hear their cries for help. The joker had to watch out when the lady got out though! All done in good fun!' 'You had to be able to take a joke,' was a recurring phrase during interviews and conversations with the women – and the men! 'Heel painting' was another long tradition that got unsuspecting victims – even foremen had to beware of this one. No one was ever supposed to have time to 'stand and talk' and those that did and were foolish enough to stand near a pit with men working in it would often walk away to be followed by loud catcalls, as the offending heels would flash bright with paint, highlighting their misdemeanour and embarrassment.

Some Works' individuals acquired a reputation of being 'a great joker'. One of those whose reputation people still recall is Ivor Mabberly, who they say was 'one of the best':

In the A Shop on some gangs there was a tradition that if you made a mistake or error in your work and were found out, word would get back to Ivor Mabberly, a man who liked to joke and fool around. One day Stan Yeates, Ray Floyd and 'Ebby' Fischer, apprentices at the time, were rebuilding axle boxes. They put the oil pipe on the wrong way round and sadly for the journeyman in charge of them, a man who was very strait-laced and meticulous in his work, it was not noticed at the time. When the inspector came to check it, he made out that he had not noticed and off he went to inform Mabberly and others. Out came the outfit for such occasions of 'dropping a clanger' – a large top hat, lots of Mayoral-type brass chains, a large red flag and a whistle. With the outfit donned and the rest of the workforce knowing, Mabberly would appear and surround the offender. Our man not knowing of his error thought it was for someone else, but no they surrounded him. The whistle was loudly blown, the flag waved and many dozens of men whooped and cheered very loudly and came from all around to mock, causing great embarrassment to the offender.

Another way of expressing their humour was in the extensive habit of nicknames. Railwaymen seemed to delight in finding 'other' names to give people and there was never a shortage of people who were never known by their real names. From Alfred Williams we learn about 'Tubby', 'about the size of a thirty-six barrel'; 'Baltimore' who dressed 'in a scarlet tunic much too big'; 'Jimmy Useless', 'a skilled workman when the spirit moved him'; 'Budget';

Maintenance fitters Andy Binks – wearing spectacular striped jumper (for a bet) – and Tony 'Puff-Puff' Pearce, next to their workbenches in 33 Shop (1981). 'Puff-Puff' got his name from his passion for steam 'puff-puff' engines, of which he built fine, detailed miniatures.

'Strawberry' and the unfortunately named 'Sambo' whose mother had been a West Indian. 'Bones', 'Kitchen', 'Blockhead', 'Swish', 'Dumpy Stumpy', 'Long Pod', 'Green Slug', 'Bucket-of-Blood', 'Noddy' and 'Nobby' are just some that Andy Binks can bring to mind during his time in the 1970s.

Sometimes these names were 'achieved' or 'acquired' through some joke or incident that took place – such was 'Drill Head' and Andy tells the story:

Melvyn, who got this nickname, was a very lucky lad to live to tell the tale. Stan Yeates and I were working high up in the foundry roof. We were working off ladders and doing the sort of stuff that Health and Safety 2008 would definitely not like. All our hand mechanical tools were pneumatic and we were using a drilling machine with the airline back to floor plugged into the air system. In the roof we had hung it over some framework for security. Stan accidentally knocked it off and it swung like a large pendulum from about 35 feet up. We both watched in horror, almost slow motion, as Melvyn, who worked on the furnaces below walked into view. The swinging heavy drilling machine hit Melvyn right on the side of

Swindon Works railwaymen had a collective identity and a collective pride. They were proud of their Works, their work and their railway heritage. Here workers commemorate their fallen colleagues at an Armistice Day service in the AE Shop. There were several 'memorials' within the Works paid for by subscriptions from the men.

the head and completely pole-axed him. We were sure we had killed him and Stan was down to the floor in seconds, with fingers crossed. A First Aider was on the scene in moments. At first Melvyn was out cold and we feared the worse. After a couple of minutes he came round, got up shakily and Stan and I breathed immense sighs of relief. Melvyn had a nasty bump on his head but hardly any blood and, fortunately never held it against either of us. That's why Melvyn was always known as … you've got it … Drill Head!

The End of the Works

Undoubtedly a 'railwayman' was a notable character. A Swindon Works' railwayman, whether of the steam or diesel era, or both, was noted by locals and worldwide. He was a complex creature, multi-layered and full of contradictions – full of pride in his work but painfully aware of his 'status' and standing; happy to be one of the gang but agonizingly aware of the need to 'fit in'; able to turn his hand to anything, anywhere, but magnetically drawn back to 'Inside' again

Bitter words. Embittered men. Some of the many slogans that appeared throughout the Works prior to closure, as Roger Hayes recalls:

> Yes I remember when the Works closed. Everybody was bitter at the time. I came to the railway works for security, the last thing I wanted was to be out of a job. My overriding memory – well, I wouldn't change my working life. I was so content. I had such fulfillment during my working career. I enjoyed everyday I went to work. I worked with a wide selection of people with lots of different sets of skills. I found it very rewarding.

and again. Even after Nationalisation he could not escape the shadow of the Great Western, for better or for worse he was stamped with 'GWR' mentality and attitude and, like the seaside rock, it went all the way through! On 26 March 1986 the Works finally closed. 1,100 workers left in disconsolate dribs and drabs as none had the heart to march out this last day with head-held-high. (450 were left to 'mop-up' over the next twelve months.) The BREL flag flew at half-mast as did the flag on St Mark's Church tower. Secretary of the Works' Committee, Terry Larkham, wore a black tie which spoke volumes about how he and the men felt. 'This is a funeral,' he told the *Swindon Advertiser*. 'The death of the Works. All are heartbroken and bitter because we had proved there was no reason to close us down.' The Works had fought its last fight ... and lost. There would be no more Swindon Works' railwaymen.

Steam was dead. Long live diesels … and for a wonderful time they did and the Works lived on, but when BR decided in favour of diesel electricals as against diesel hydraulics, it was the beginning of a long, slow, painful end for Swindon Works. 'Last Man Standing' machinist Norman 'Jock' Taylor stands guard over his shaping machine, as the shops are cleared for closure, trying to come to terms with what this means for his (and his mates') future. Like all the men, he did not understand why or how it came to this. Andy Bink recalls:

> Taking this photograph gave me a complete reality check. I stood there thinking, "this really is the end. The fun, the frolics, the laughter, even the tears, would soon be at an end. There'd be no more talking, no more hoping. What would I do? Would life go on nicely? Would it get tough or be the same?"
> For me, things got better (and better paid) and now this once-thriving, happy workplace is a distant memory and the place where Jock stood has become a well-known brand shop in a retail village.

Endnotes

1.   Matheson, Thesis.

2.   Swindon.

3.   Quotes from *The Daily Chronicle*, December 1812, Jan/Feb/March/ June 1913, as seen in Churchward's Cuttings Diary in STEAM and outlined in Matheson thesis.

The Works is dead … and gone. Long live its memory and that of all the boys, men and women who worked in its workshops. (P1 Shop 1986 taken by Andy Binks.)

Bibliography

Ball Felicity & Bryan Tim, *Swindon and the GWR*, Tempus Publishing Ltd, 2003

Bryan, Tim *The Golden Age of the Great Western 1895-1914*, Patrick Stephens, 1991, and *Great Western Swindon*, The Chalford Publishing Co., 1995

Butler, Stuart, *Who Says There's No Poetry In Swindon?*

Chandler, John, *Swindon Decoded*, Hobnob Press, 2005

Cockbill, Trevor, *Finest Thing Out: The Story of the Mechanics' Institute at New Swindon 1843–1873*, The Quill Press, Swindon, 1988, and *Our Swindon in 1939*, Quill Press, Swindon, 1989, 2nd Edition, The Mechanics' Institute Preservation Trust Ltd, 1999

Crittal, Elizabeth, K.H. Rogers and Colin Shrimpton, *A History of Swindon to 1965*, Institute of Historical Research & Wiltshire Library & Museum Service, Trowbridge, 1983. This book was reprinted from *The Victoria County History of Wiltshire Volume IX*

Darwin, Bernard, *A Century of Medical Service: The Story of the Great Western Railway Medical Fund Society 1847 to 1947*, The GWR Medical Fund Society, Swindon, 1947

Durrant A.E., *Swindon Apprentice, An Inside Portrait of the Great Western Locomotive Works*, Runpast Publishing, 1989

Hudson, John & Linda, *In The News – Swindon*, Sutton Publishing Ltd, 2002

Ellis, Hamilton, *British Railway History 1877-1947*, George Allen & Unwin Ltd, 1959

Freebury, Hugh, *Great Western Apprentice, Swindon in the thirties*, Wiltshire County Council Library & Museum Services, 1985

Gibbs, Ken, *Swindon Works: Apprentice in Steam*, Oxford Publishing Co., 1986

Hudson, Kenneth, *Working to Rule: Railway Workshop Rules: A Study of Industrial Discipline*, Adams & Dart, 1970

Larkin, Eric, *An Illustrated History of British Railways Workshops*, Oxford Publishing Co., 1992

Measom, George, *The Illustrated Guide to The Great Western Railway*, W. Marshall & Sons, 1852.

Mountford, Eric R., *Swindon, GWR Reminiscences*, Bradford Barton Ltd

Peck, Alan, *The Great Western at Swindon Works*, The Oxford Publishing Company, 1983

Platt, Alan, *The Life and Times of Daniel Gooch*, Alan Sutton, 1987

Silto, Joseph, *A Swindon History 1840–1901*, 1981

Simmons, Jack, *The Railways of Britain. A Journey Through History*, Macmillan Ltd, 1986

Wells, H.B., *Swindon in the 19th and 20th Centuries* and John Betjeman, *Architecture* in *Studies in the History of Swindon,* L.V. Grinsell *et al*, Swindon Borough Council, 1950

Unacknowledged, *The Town and Works of Swindon with a Brief History of the Broad Gauge*, Victoria Press, 1892

Academic Thesis and Papers

Attwell, Graham, Paper: *Rediscovering Apprenticeship? A Historical Approach*, 1997

Eversley, D.E.C. *The Great Western Railway and Swindon Works in the Great Depression*. Historical Journal V, 1957

Matheson, Rosa, *Women and The Great Western Railway with Specific Reference to Swindon Works.* Doctorate thesis, University of the West of England, 2002

Pierce, Jackie, *Corpus Sanem, Mentem Senem: A Study of Victorian Paternalism in Swindon and London.* BA (Hons) Combined Studies Dissertation, Bath College of Higher Education, 1995

Newspapers and Journals

Astill's Local Directory

The Great Western Railway Magazine

The Railway Gazette

The Daily Chronicle

The Evening Advertiser

The Swindon Advertiser

The Wiltshire Gazette & Herald

If you are interested in purchasing other books published by The History Press,
or in case you have difficulty finding any History Press books in your local bookshop,
you can also place orders directly through our website

www.thehistorypress.co.uk